# STOCKHOLM

A pocket guide to the city's best
cultural hangouts, shops, bars
and eateries

**BECKY OHLSEN**

Hardie Grant
TRAVEL

# CONTENTƧ

# INTRODUCTION

Stockholm is a visual delight, both in the way it's situated – spread across 14 islands, its precincts are often literally defined by water – and because of its trademark Swedish design. Public spaces are designed and lit to cinematic perfection; the average person on the street looks like (and is likely to be) a fashion social-media influencer; and even humble cafes have perfect lighting and enviable furnishings. Everything looks art-directed, down to the tunnelbana (train) stations.

Walking around Stockholm, it's hard not to be struck by something gorgeous every time you turn a corner. Years ago, after a last-minute decision to attend a Christmas concert inside a church dating from the 1600s, my parents and I stepped outside into the falling snow just as the royal palace guard, complete with marching band, launched its procession towards the palace, over a medieval bridge and into Gamla Stan (Old Town). This moment is typical of the city's magic.

Some moments of Stockholm's beauty are quieter: catching the last rays of golden sunlight glittering across the water as you walk along the cliffs of Södermalm; noticing an ancient runestone embedded in the corner of a building; stretching out your arms to touch the red-and-ochre buildings on either side of a narrow cobblestone street, then looking up at a slice of blue sky between them; stopping for a break in a square where shiny modern buildings frame statues of water sprites; and feeling astounded all over again at the effortless style of the beautiful people around you.

But the city's appeal goes beyond surface level. The food is spectacular, particularly in recent years, thanks to the welcome influence of immigrant cultures and the dedication to using hyperlocal, seasonal, sustainably produced ingredients. Stores are inspired design spaces. Museums and cultural attractions are must-sees: uniformly well-funded, high-quality, interactive and informative. Everywhere you go, green spaces abound and people spend time in them.

*Stockholm Pocket Precincts* takes you to nine of the city's precincts and beyond into the archipelago, to Drottningholm Palace and to the university city of Uppsala. Immerse yourself and see why Stockholm is a place to be inspired – with a view at every turn.

**Becky Ohlsen**

# A PERFECT ∫TOCKHOLM DAY

Stockholm is not a crack-of-dawn city. A perfect day here begins *slowly*. Nothing much is open before about 10am, which means early risers have the streets all to themselves.

I'm mildly obsessed with the buffet at the design-forward **Hotel C**, right next to the airport express train station. Here you can stroll around with a tray and gather: hardbread, flatbread, dark rye, baguette, cheese, cold-cuts, yoghurt, muesli and fruit, topped off with pancakes or scrambled eggs and bacon. Oh, and lots of coffee, bitter and strong.

After breakfast, walk to Gamla Stan (Old Town), the city's historic core, with its tangle of winding cobblestone streets and tall, slouching buildings. Plan on getting lost but do make a point to find **Stortorget**, the pretty main square. Pick up some locally made, handcrafted keepsakes and artwork at **Studio Lena M** or **Hilda Hilda**. And it's never too early for a scoop of quintessentially Swedish saffron-honey ice-cream from one of the shops on Västerlånggatan or a 'mumma' cake at **Grillska Husets Konditori**.

From Gamla Stan, navigate the complicated traffic hub called Slussen (it's under construction from now until forever, so you'll have to follow signs along temporary footpaths) to reach Södermalm, the southernmost island. Walk along the water's edge or take the tunnelbana (train) west to Hornstull. Stop for lunch (or, if it's too early, pick up a healthy sandwich or salad to go) at neighbourhood favourite **Vurma**. A pedestrian walkway connects Hornstull to tiny Långholmen; beside the bridge is **Långholmen Kajak**, where you can rent a canoe or kayak and paddle the canals all through the city, perhaps stopping at one of the small inviting beaches on Långholmen or Kungsholmen to enjoy your picnic lunch and take a swim.

Post-paddle, grab a coffee and pastry (the beloved Swedish coffee break, called fika) at leafy green **Lasse i Parken**. Hop on the tunnelbana to **Medborgarplatsen**, Södermalm's busy central square. Explore the shops and bars of Södermalm's 'SoFo' (South of Folkungagatan), especially the lifestyle and household goods store **Grandpa**. Play some pinball at the charming adult game centre **Ugglan**, and wrap up with a visit to **Fotografiska**, the photo museum – it's open late and has a cool terrace bar. Then ascend the cobbled streets up to **Hermans** vegetarian restaurant, high above Fotografiska, for dinner with a view.

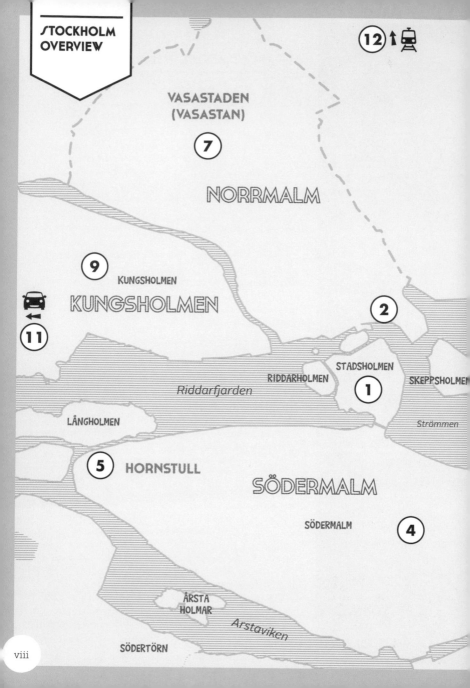

STOCKHOLM
OVERVIEW

(12)

VASASTADEN
(VASASTAN)

(7)

NORRMALM

(9)

KUNGSHOLMEN

KUNGSHOLMEN

(2)

(11)

STADSHOLMEN

RIDDARHOLMEN

SKEPPSHOLMEN

(1)

Riddarfjarden

Strömmen

LÅNGHOLMEN

(5)  HORNSTULL

SÖDERMALM

SÖDERMALM

(4)

ÅRSTA
HOLMAR

Arstaviken

SÖDERTÖRN

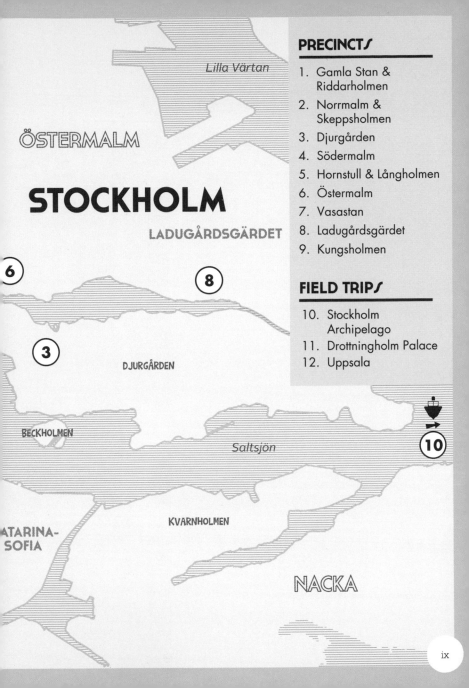

ÖSTERMALM

# STOCKHOLM

LADUGÅRDSGÄRDET

*Lilla Värtan*

DJURGÅRDEN

BECKHOLMEN

*Saltsjön*

KVARNHOLMEN

ATARINA-
SOFIA

NACKA

# GAMLA STAN & RIDDARHOLMEN

It's hard not to swoon over Stockholm's Gamla Stan (Old Town), a tiny island crammed with saffron-and-spice-coloured medieval buildings sagging toward each other across narrow cobblestone streets. The city was founded here in 1252. It is home to the Royal Palace, the Nobel Museum, and Stockholm's narrowest street. Stortorget (see p. 2), the main square at the heart of the island, is lined with adorable cafes. Most visitors stick to three main streets: busy Stora Nygatan, pedestrianised Västerlånggatan and slightly quieter Österlånggatan, both of which originally ran just outside the city walls. Following the herd is fine, but it's more fun to get happily lost – grab an exotic-sounding flavour of ice-cream from one of several cafes (black licorice, anyone?) and wander down any skinny alleyway that beckons, including the 90-centimetre wide Mårten Trotzigs gränd. You'll quickly leave the souvenir shops behind, and with a little imagination you can pretend you're time-travelling. (Don't worry, though – the island is tiny, and walking in any direction will soon get you back to a main street.)

Linked to Gamla Stan by bridge, the jewelbox islet of Riddarholmen (meaning 'the Knights' Island'), is home to Riddarholms Kyrkan (see p. 4), the city's most striking church. It's surrounded by huge 17th-century pink and white palaces. The views from here are epic, and you can circle the islet on foot in minutes.

Tunnelbana: Gamla Stan

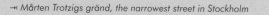
→ Mårten Trotzigs gränd, the narrowest street in Stockholm

**SIGHTS**
1. Stortorget (Main Square)
2. Livrustkammaren (Royal Armoury)
3. Riddarholms Kyrkan

**SHOPPING**
4. Studio Lena M
5. Iris Hantverk
6. Hilda Hilda
7. Kerstin Adolphson Butik

**EATING & DRINKING**
8. Wirströms Pub
9. Grillska Husets Konditori
10. Under Kastanjen

# 1 STORTORGET (MAIN SQUARE)

Gamla Stan
Open daily 24-hrs
[MAP p. 141 D3]

The old town's main square is the precinct's adorable cobblestone heart. It's lined with cafes in colourful historic buildings with elaborate roof-lines and decorative facades. The fountain in its centre is from 1778 but a well has stood here since the Middle Ages, marking the official centre of town. In fair weather, cafes such as **Grillska Husets Konditori** (*see* p. 8) have outdoor seating; when temperatures drop, you can duck into a candlelit cellar room. The **Nobel Museum** gives you a history of the coveted prize and is housed in the neoclassical former Stock Exchange building, built in the 1770s. History buffs know the square as the site of the Stockholm Bloodbath of November 1520. To squelch resistance by Swedes who wanted independence from the Kalmar Union and Danish rule, the Danish king Christian II invited more than 80 Swedish nobles to the palace and then had them hanged or beheaded in the square. This sparked Sweden's war for independence. But these days the square is peaceful and cheery.

**POCKET TIP**
The narrowest street in Stockholm, Mårten Trotzigs gränd, is an almost mandatory selfie stop – look for it between Västerlånggatan and Prästgatan.

## 2 LIVRUSTKAMMAREN (ROYAL ARMOURY)

Slottsbacken 3
08 402 30 30
livrustkammaren.se
Open Tues–Sun 10am–6pm
(Jul–Aug), 11am–5pm
(Sept–Jun)
[MAP p. 141 E1, 145 C4]

The Royal Armoury, occupying the basement vaults of the royal palace, is the oldest museum in Sweden and full of fascinating artefacts. There's a parade of royal costumes from over the centuries (some of them still mud- and blood-splattered, commemorating valour or misfortune), a stash of weapons from Stockholm's original Three Crowns palace (which burned down in 1697), and a beautiful collection of impossibly delicate, elaborately gilded coaches and carriages. But the popular favourite here is the stuffed horse Streiff, the steed that King Gustav II Adolf was riding when he was killed in the Battle of Lützen in 1632. The permanent collection has been expanded and the space renovated as of 2019. Admission is free to the main hall (there's occasionally a charge for a temporary exhibit); the entrance is along the southeast wall of the palace at ground level.

**POCKET TIP**

Skip the royal palace tour in favour of the free Changing of the Guard in the outdoor courtyard (12.15pm Mon–Sat, 1.15pm Sun and holidays).

3

# 3 RIDDARHOLMS KYRKAN

Riddarholmen
08 402 61 00
www.kungligaslotten.se
Open daily 10am–5pm
(May–Sept)
[MAP p. 140 A3]

One of my favourite elements of the Stockholm skyline, the Riddarholm church's cast-iron spire (visible from all over town) sticks up into what always seems like a cloudy sky, even when the sun is shining elsewhere in the city. Or maybe I just see it that way because I know what's inside: this gloomy church is home to the royal crypt, where all the Swedish monarchs from medieval times to the 1950s ended up. (The one exception is lifelong non-conformist Queen Christina, buried in Rome at St Peter's Basilica.) From June through August there are guided tours in English daily at 2.30pm; join one of these if you can, as it gets you into the crypts where guides share gossipy stories about the occupants – including King Waldemar, son of historic Stockholm statesman Birger Jarl (both names are ubiquitous). Worn stone stairs lead to the vault, with its gold-starred ceiling over elaborately gilded and decorated coffins. Riddarholms Kyrkan is rarely open in winter.

**POCKET TIP**
For stellar views over Lake Mälaren, head to Evert Taube's terrace and namesake statue at Riddarholmen's west edge.

# 4 STUDIO LENA M

Kindstugan 14
0708 842 892
studiolenam.wordpress.com
Open Mon–Fri 10am–6pm,
Sat 10am–3pm
[MAP p. 141 E3]

This little shop, tucked away on a side street, provides the opposite experience to the usual souvenir shopping in Gamla Stan. There are no plastic Viking helmets or wooden-horse refrigerator magnets here. The tiny space is done up in reclaimed and recycled materials, and artist Lena M is often behind the counter. Her simple but adorable designs on serving trays and dish cloths make ideal gifts to take home: choose from beautiful motifs of fish, birds, moose and other animals or iconic Stockholm buildings. Not only are they unique, practical and *very* Swedish, but they weigh nothing and are easy to pack. Lena also creates beautiful paintings on recycled wood. You can be happy knowing you're directly supporting a local artist.

# 5 IRIS HANTVERK

Västerlånggatan 24
08 698 09 73
www.irishantverk.se
Open Mon–Fri 10am–6pm,
Sat 10am–3pm
[MAP p. 140 C3]

Known for its ultra-soft handmade wooden brushes and beautiful textiles, this store – with a few locations around town – also stocks carefully chosen household goods and handicrafts of a uniformly high quality. Think sturdy wooden toys, kitchen gadgets that are too pretty to use, unbelievably soft towels and luxurious throw blankets. All of it is genuinely well made and there's a bonus: Iris Hantverk works primarily with artisans and suppliers who are visually impaired. The company got its start with a half-dozen visually impaired craftspeople making one-of-a-kind wooden brushes in a traditional Swedish style, then gradually expanded its offerings over the years. With its soft lighting and meticulously organised blonde-wood shelves, the shop is a soothing, pleasant place even if you're just browsing.

## 6 HILDA HILDA

Österlånggatan 21
08 641 36 80
www.hildahilda.se
Open Mon–Fri 10am–6pm, Sat
10am–4pm, Sun 11am–4pm
[MAP p. 141 F3]

You *need* a throw pillow with a dachshund on it and also a matching pencil case in the same material with a smaller version of the same dachshund. And also a glasses case with a picture of eyeglasses woven into it, a breakfast serving tray with half a hard-boiled egg on it, and a pot-holder in the shape of a fish. Hilda Hilda makes some of the most whimsical textiles and textile-based household goods, from tote bags and pillows to table runners and make-up cases, sold in this tiny shop where you can often see a craftsperson at work in the back room. Their products are both totally original and quintessentially Swedish.

# 7 KERSTIN ADOLPHSON BUTIK

Västerlånggatan 40
08 20 17 27
Open Mon–Fri 10am–6pm,
Sat 10am–4pm, Sun
11am–4pm
[MAP p. 141 D3]

The thing is, it's hard not to be tempted to shop for souvenirs and gifts as you roam the streets of Gamla Stan, but you don't want to buy a bunch of junk you'll later regret. This shop, right in the middle of the pedestrian thoroughfare, has the national blue and yellow costumes in the window but it also carries other high-quality Scandinavian goods, such as soft Norwegian fisherman's sweaters, cute and comfy painted clogs, and those great pointy-fingered woollen gloves and thick wool socks that say 'I'll never forget that time I survived a Nordic winter.' Look for traditional Indigenous Sami silver-filigreed bracelets, ultra-cosy house slippers and leather handbags, too.

## POCKET TIP

Head to Café Järntorget (Västerlånggatan 81) for saffron–honey ice-cream and other quintessentially Swedish flavours.

# 8 WIRSTRÖMS PUB

Stora Nygatan 13
08 21 28 74
www.wirstromspub.se
Open Mon–Wed 2pm–12am,
Sun & Thurs–Fri 12pm–12am,
Sat 11am–12am
[MAP p. 140 C3]

This is the pub that never ends and they should almost hand out a map when you order. At first, it looks just like any old Irish pub that isn't in Ireland: Guinness on tap, expats in the booths all watching football matches, bartender with an Irish-enough accent. But this pub is in Gamla Stan, which means it has underground vaults and cellars that go on and on, so you can carry your Guinness and your conversation into the deepest, darkest corners of the labyrinth downstairs. It's all candlelit and mysterious with books, occasionally a second bar, and sometimes even live music, so don't be shy. But if you send a friend back upstairs for another round, and it takes her an unusually long time to bring the drinks back, well, you'd better make new friends, because she's probably lost.

## 9 GRILLSKA HUSETS KONDITORI

Stortorget 3
08 684 23 364
www.stadsmissionen.se/vad-vi-gor/grillska-huset
Open Mon 10am–7pm,
Tues–Sat 10am–9pm, Sun
11am–7pm
[MAP p. 141 D3]

Sure, if you want to be seen, go across the square to the pair of cafes occupying the ground floor of two iconic Old Town buildings. But you should go to this humble cafe instead, for several reasons: one, it's less crowded; two, the food is better value; three, you get to actually *look* at those buildings while you eat; and four, the baked goods here are amazing. Reason five is the main reason though: Grillska Huset's specialty 'mumma' cakes – dense, eggy little almond–cardamom bombs that were invented here. They come in two sizes; get the large, and get several. You won't regret it. Come for the daily lunch special and grab a seat on the outdoor patio. Afterwards, duck into the bakery to load up on take-away treats. Best of all, your lunch money benefits Stockholms Stadsmission, a charity organisation that runs the cafe.

Citronmaräng    45:- / 49:-

45:- / 49:-

16-18

18 Lock

# 10 UNDER KASTANJEN

Kindstugatan 1
08 21 50 04
www.underkastanjen.se
Open Mon–Fri 8am–11pm, Sat
9am–11pm, Sun 9am–9pm
[MAP p. 141 E3]

At some point on any trip to Stockholm, you really should sit down for a plate of Swedish meatballs, traditionally made with beef and pork (and sometimes veal) and served with mashed potato, gravy and lingonberries. This low-key but pretty spot in a tree-lined courtyard is one of the more comfortable (and affordable) places to do that – its daily lunch specials are all about husmanskost, or humble (though elevated) traditional Swedish home cooking, and meatballs are a permanent menu item. Other good choices include any of the soups, baked salmon and sirloin steak – and potatoes with everything. As the day goes on, the cafe turns into a wine bar, with a super-romantic little outdoor courtyard. In between, it's great for coffee and pastries.

# NORRMALM &
# SKEPPSHOLMEN

Norrmalm is the functional if not quite geographical centre of Stockholm, a traveller precinct and where some of the city's most important hubs of activity are. Most people visiting the city inevitably start here: it's home to the central bus, train and tunnelbana (train) stations, where all the various transport lines through the city converge, including the express train from Arlanda Airport (see p. 132). Norrmalm also has the highest concentration of hotel rooms and other traveller services, like car-rental companies, banks and tourist information offices. This might make it sound like it's all business, but some of the city's liveliest public squares are also here – notably Kungsträdgården (The King's Garden, or 'Kungsan' to locals, see p. 23), Hötorget (Haymarket Square), a wide cobblestone square with a daily farmers' market, and Sergels Torg (see p. 19), which hosts public events. On its south side is Kulturhuset, a cultural centre in an award-winning (but, to some, architecturally controversial) building. On the surrounding streets you'll find the full spectrum of Stockholm's restaurants, bars and shops. Drottninggatan, the main pedestrian thoroughfare, runs the souvenir-shop gauntlet into Gamla Stan (Old Town).

Connected by a footbridge to Norrmalm's south-eastern corner, Skeppsholmen has outstanding views of the skyline across the water, plus Moderna Museet (Modern Art Museum, see p. 16), the one place I never fail to visit.

Bus, tunnelbana, tram: T-Centralen, Kungsträdgården, Hötorget

→ *Kajsas Fisk serves giant bowls of seafood stew in an underground food market*

# 1 MODERNA MUSEET (MODERN ART MUSEUM)

Exercisplan 4
08 520 235 00
www.modernamuseet.se
Open Tues 10am–8pm,
Wed–Thurs 10am–6pm,
Fri 10am–8pm, Sat–Sun
11am–6pm
[MAP p. 146 A2]

'You don't have to like every painting,' my grandfather told me once on a visit to Moderna, 'but you should think about how to become friends with each of them.' He was an artist and an art critic for Stockholm's daily paper and I loved hearing him talk about art. And I listened: I have since become good friends with most of the pieces in Moderna Museet's permanent collection. I visit them often, and I have my favourites: Giacomo Balla's almost-in-motion Futurist painting *Speed of a Car + Light*; Robert Rauschenburg's *Monogram* (aka the Goat in the Tire); the whole Marcel Duchamp-Dadaist room; and, best of all, Swedish artist Öyvind Fahlström's enormous, ultra-precise comics-style canvases. The museum's temporary exhibits are also consistently excellent.

The **Moderna Museet Restaurant** has epic views across the water to Djurgården and a hearty daily lunch. **Cafe Blom** has humbler options.

## POCKET TIP

Attached to Moderna is the Design and Architecture Museum, ArkDes, which has temporary exhibits, such as the history of the city's architecture and planning.

## 2 MEDELHAVSMUSEET (MEDITERRANEAN MUSEUM)

Fredsgatan 2
010 456 12 98
www.varldskulturmuseerna.se/
medelhavsmuseet
Open Tues–Fri 11am–8pm,
Sat–Sun 11am–5pm
[MAP p. 145 A2]

Maybe it sounds odd to recommend a Mediterranean museum to visitors to Sweden or even to have a Mediterranean museum in Sweden but this place quickly dispels any doubts. The main hall has the feel of an Italianate mansion, with pillars, colonnades and elegant marble statues everywhere. Except there are also these bright-green, shiny, trapezoidal shapes in the middle of the room, dividing and confusing the space and letting you know this isn't just any old mansion. The shapes turn out to be display cases, holding collections of artefacts from all over the Mediterranean – Bronze Age pottery excavated from tombs in Cyprus, Greek vases collected by King Gustav III and 7th-century Islamic art – along with detailed explanations of what they are and why they matter. (And yes, there are mummies.) **Bagdad Café** is a great option for a healthy Mediterranean lunch; try the feta-eggplant salad or spicy lamb meatballs.

# 3 SVENSK HEMSLÖJD

Norrlandsgatan 20
08 23 21 15
svenskhemslojd.com
Open Mon–Fri 10am–6pm, Sat
11am–4pm, Sun 12pm–4pm
[MAP p. 143 D2]

If you want to be sure that the handicrafts you're buying are the absolutely best possible quality, this is the place to shop. Hemslöjd means handicraft, and the artisans here are part of a collective with extremely high standards for quality and authenticity. Things are made traditionally, not mass-produced. (And if you have a craftsperson in your life, this is *the* place to pick up super-luxurious yarns and how-to books). Look especially for textiles of all kinds, from table runners and kitchen towels to rugs and pillow cases; hand-woven wool clothing; painted wooden horses from Dalarna; Indigenous Sami jewellery; adorable quilted pot-holders; and beautifully carved wooden kitchen tools. They're not all cheap, but you're buying quality and supporting Sweden's makers.

**POCKET TIP**

After lengthy renovations, the Nationalmuseum (National Gallery) has reopened with centuries' worth of painting, sculpture and applied arts, including several masterpieces.

## 4 DESIGNTORGET

Sergelgången 29
08 21 91 50
www.designtorget.se
Open Mon–Fri 10am–8pm, Sat
10am–7pm, Sun 11am–6pm
[MAP p. 142 B4]

You love IKEA but this is nicer and way cheaper than the big-name design stores (which, in Stockholm, might as well be museums). Designtorget provides an outlet for up-and-coming designers as well as established names, specialising in examples of brilliant Swedish design. Here you might pick up an early version of household items by the next big name designer. Everything is cleverly made, whether it's a cheese grater, a towel hook, a serving tray or a bookshelf. Look for kids' toys, candle holders, easily packable kitchen linens, art books and any number of other things you didn't know you needed. This is a good place to shop for your last-minute gifts, especially because there are locations all over town. (This one is very central; there's another inside Central Station).

**POCKET TIP**

Sergels Torg is a multi-level space with a big glass obelisk in the middle. It often hosts public speakers, political demonstrations and other gatherings.

# 5 NK (NORDISKA KOMPANIET)

Hamngatan 18–20
08 762 80 00
www.nk.se
Open Mon–Fri 10am–8pm, Sat 10am–6pm, Sun 11am–5pm
[MAP p. 142 C3]

As much a cathedral of commerce as a department store, NK is beloved among Stockholmers for a few things in particular: one, its hotdogs (grillad korv), which are probably no better than any other hotdog on any Stockholm street, but these are *from NK*, so … you know. Two, the annual holiday window displays – every December, each of the store's big windows is transformed into its own little wintery world, with elaborate props, lighting and animatronic figures doing entrancing things. People line up to look at them (me too). But for most visitors, NK is all about the basement: a treasure chest of good-quality, reasonably priced, authentic Swedish gifts. Even the simplest household items boast superb Scandinavian design – from glassware and crystal to textiles, napkins and wooden knives. If you've put off your shopping to the last minute, do it here. The customer service department is generous with advice on tax-free shopping and on the best way to safely pack your gifts for transport.

**POCKET TIP**
Most Swedish glassware comes from the Kingdom of Crystal, a cluster of glasswork factories in the southern province of Småland.

**POCKET TIP**

Hotel C has cleverly designed pocket-size budget rooms, a vast breakfast buffet and the kitschy Ice Bar, where you bundle up and drink from ice glasses.

# 6 WIENER CAFÉET

Biblioteksgatan 6–8
08 684 23 850
wienercafeet.com
Open Mon 7am–7pm, Tues–Fri
7am–9pm, Sat 9.30am–9pm,
Sun 9.30am–7pm
[MAP p. 143 D2]

Spiritually this beautiful cafe
might be considered more
a part of Östermalm, but
technically it's just across the
imaginary line in Norrmalm.
Inspired by the grandeur
of Viennese and Parisian
salons, without being snooty,
the entire place is achingly
beautiful, from the pastries and
cakes to the giant windows
and the carved wooden details
inside. (Was it once a jewellery
shop? It's that pretty, but
somehow I've never asked).
Menu items range from eggs
Benedict to roasted-root-
vegetable salads and beyond,
and it's all several notches
better than what a cafe lunch
needs to be. Wait staff wear
black tie but you don't have
to, although you might feel like
dressing up if you turn up for
the elaborate afternoon tea.

**POCKET TIP**

Sample Scandinavian
cuisine at Smaka på
Stockholm (A Taste of
Stockholm), held the first
week of June each year
in Kungsträdgården.

## 7 HOLY GREEN∫

Regeringsgatan 28
08 22 62 22
www.holygreens.se
Open Mon–Fri 8am–7pm,
Sat–Sun 11am–5pm
[MAP p. 142 C4, 143 D2]

Holy Greens will save you.
Discovering this place a couple
of years ago made me so
happy. Because sometimes you
just don't want to spend two
hours sitting in a restaurant
for lunch, but nor do you want
a fast-food cheeseburger or
the gross Swedish version
of pizza (sorry, it's true). The
concept here is simple: various
combinations of superfoods
and healthy proteins in bowls,
assembled as you order, to
go or to eat in its elegantly
spartan dining room. It's
super-fast and still pretty
cheap, for Stockholm. You can
also get fruit smoothies, fresh
juices and coffee (of course).
Any of the bowls with salmon
or the seasonal special is a
good bet.

**POCKET TIP**
At Kungsträdgården
you can ice-skate
in the winter and
attend festivals and
cultural events in
the summer.

# 8 KAJSAS FISK

Hötorgshallen Food Market,
Hötorget
08 20 72 62
kajsasfisk.com
Open Mon–Thurs 11am–6pm,
Fri 11am–7pm, Sat 11am–4pm
[MAP p. 142 A2]

This is one of my favourite
Stockholm rituals: on a cold
day, or really any day after
walking around the city, I'll
head underground to the food
market inside Hötorgshallen.
In the tiniest back corner
is a little galleon-shaped
fish restaurant, one of my
grandmother's regular lunch
spots (although she would
always go late, close to 4pm,
to avoid a wait). Everything
on the menu is perfect – it
comes straight from the fresh-
fish counter next-door – but
I always order the enormous
bowl of fish soup, scooped out
of a vast tureen and topped
with aioli. It's crammed with
salmon, prawns, mussels and
whatever other exotic sea
creatures turned up in the
day's catch; served with bread
and salad, maybe a glass of
white wine if you're feeling
decadent, it'll warm you for the
rest of the day.

**HÖTORGSHALLEN**

## POCKET TIP

It doesn't get much
love in print, but the
traditional open shrimp
sandwich (räksmörgås)
is a reliably delicious
lunch favourite.

# 9 OPERAN (ROYAL OPERA)

Karl XII's torg
08 676 58 08
www.operan.se (Opera), www.
operakallaren.se (restaurants),
www.cafeopera.se (nightclub)
Bakfickan open: Mon–Thurs
11.30am–10pm, Fri 11.30am–
11pm, Sat 12pm–11pm, Sun
12pm–5pm; Café Opera open:
Wed–Sun 10pm–3am
[MAP p. 145 B2]

It's not so much the opera as the many decadent bars and restaurants in the Royal Opera building that make Stockholmers talk about this must-visit highbrow entertainment complex. The main dining room attached to the opera house, **Operakällaren**, is an exclusive Michelin-starred restaurant in an utterly gorgeous space – I suggest peeking inside if it's open. More accessible is the 'hip pocket' restaurant, **Bakfickan**, with a menu of perfectly executed (but not outrageous) traditional Swedish dishes, such as herring and meatballs, in an intimate '60s-style room with counter seating (no reservations, so just try your luck). Finally, the decadent **Café Opera** has a permanent space on every list of nightclub hot spots in Stockholm, with DJs and dance nights on a rotating schedule.

**POCKET TIP**

If you're under age 26, you can get opera tickets for 50 per cent off. Under 40? That means 40 per cent off on tickets to the most-performed operas.

# DJURGÅRDEN

When you look at this serene island today, it's hard to picture royalty prowling the woods, hunting for game. But that's how it was in Djurgården's early days. Modern visitors will have to settle for counting tourists instead but don't let the crowds discourage you. There are plenty of worthy sights to visit: this is the home of most of Stockholm's big-ticket museums and attractions. Especially in summer when the corner of Djurgården nearest the city centre constantly swarms with people making their way to the home of the salvaged 17th-century *Vasa* warship (*see* p. 30), the mini Sweden at the Skansen museum (*see* p. 32) or the Abba Museum (*see* p. 30), ice-cream and hotdogs in hand.

Be sure to venture further, to the quiet green outskirts of the island, where the main activities are strolling or cycling along canalside paths and enjoying a picnic or an excellent meal in a unique setting. I recommend borrowing or hiring a bicycle to explore the island as much as you like. Wander far enough and you can easily find a corner all to yourself.

Ferry, bus, tram: Skansen (Djurgården ferry, Bus 67, Tram 7)

→ *Despite its many tourist attractions, Djurgården is a quiet green oasis*

**SIGHTS**
1. Vasa Museet
   (Vasa Museum)
2. Skansen
3. Spritmuseum
4. Nordiska Museet
   (Nordic Museum)
5. Prins Eugens
   Waldemarsudde
6. Thielska Galleriet
   (The Thiel Gallery)

**EATING**
7. Rosendals
   Trädgårdskafé
8. Oaxen Krog & Slip

# 1 VASA MUSEET (VASA MUSEUM)

Galärvarvsvägen 14
08 519 548 80
www.vasamuseet.se
Open daily 8.30am–6pm
(June–Aug), 10am–5pm (Sept–
May) (to 8pm Wed year-round)
[MAP p. 146 C2, 149 B4]

A rare example of a tourist attraction that lives up to the hype, the Vasa Museum is one place every Stockholmer will recommend to visitors. It's a purpose-built museum housing the intact *Vasa* war ship, a catastrophic failure (er ... *lesson*). Billed as the most powerful war ship in the Baltic, the *Vasa* set sail on 10 August 1628 – only to capsize and sink within minutes. Thirty people died, many more were embarrassed, and the ship was lost to the sea for hundreds of years. An amateur archaeologist found it in the 1950s, starting a lengthy process of rescue and restoration. It's now the only example of an entire 17th-century ship ever salvaged. The *Vasa* grabs you for its sheer scale, the ambition of the shipbuilders, the characters unlucky enough to be on board and how it went wrong. One evocative section describes the dangerous process of salvaging the ship: tunnelling under, then wrapping it in cables to lift it slowly out of the water.

**POCKET TIP**
Fans of the famed Swedish pop group won't want to miss ABBA: The Museum (Djurgårdsvägen 68), with interactive, multimedia exhibits.

# 2 SKANSEN

Djurgårdsslätten 49–51
08 442 82 00
www.skansen.se
Open daily 10am–4pm
(longer hours in summer)
[MAP p. 147 E3]

This open-air museum on a hill is 'Sweden in miniature', but it feels enormous. Bring snacks, wear comfortable shoes and spend a full day exploring. Museum mastermind Artur Hazelius founded it in 1891 to bring together the folk traditions of all of Sweden's various far-flung provinces. Historic buildings from the northern- and southern-most points in the country were moved here (including a Sami Indigenous camp). Volunteers in traditional costumes explain what life was like at that time and place. In spring, the **Nordic Zoo** rewards you with adorable baby versions of Scandinavia's many native species: bear cubs, piglets, lambs, tiny reindeer. Make sure not to miss the **glassblowers' workshop**, a small wooden hut in which master glassmakers conduct fascinating demonstrations (enter through the gift shop). If you're looking for traditional Swedish souvenirs, the **gift shop** has high-quality crafts at decent prices. Visit the **bakery** in another tiny wooden house, for traditional Swedish goodies and breads.

## 3 SPRITMUSEUM

Djurgårdsvägen 38–40
08 121 313 00
spritmuseum.se
Open Mon–Tues 10am–5pm,
Wed–Sat 10am–7pm, Sun
12pm–5pm
Restaurant open museum hours
and until late Thurs–Sat
[MAP p. 146 C2]

Booze is a fraught topic in Sweden and this museum about its history and cultural significance does a great job of digging into why and how. Housed in a stylish building, the collection is displayed with a healthy splash of grim Scandinavian humour. The hangover room demonstrates paying dearly for your excesses; it's a cramped closet-size apartment with bad lighting and a low buzzing noise that slowly increases to headache-inducing levels. Next to that is a small theatre to imitate tipsiness: in hazy blue light, you lie back on sofas and watch a tilted screen showing increasingly drunk people walking and talking. You can listen to recorded drinking songs, sniff the aromas of various styles of aquavit in a 'nose organ' and take a pub quiz to test your alcohol knowledge. Wrap up your visit with a tasting tray of three aquavit samples and a Swedish punsch in the foyer bar.

## 4 NORDISKA MUSEET (NORDIC MUSEUM)

Djurgårdsvägen 6–16
08 519 547 70
www.nordiskamuseet.se
Open daily 9am–6pm
(Jun–Aug), Thurs–Tues
10am–5pm, Wed 10am–8pm
(Sept–May)
[MAP p. 146 C1, 149 B4]

This museum, created by
Artur Hazelius in 1873, is an
enormous compendium of
Nordic cultural artefacts inside
a striking faux-Renaissance-
palace building. The best thing
is what you see when you
walk through the big wooden
doors: a giant oak statue of
the Father of Sweden, Gustav
Vasa. He was king from 1523 to
1560 and led Sweden's war for
independence from Denmark.
Beloved Swedish sculptor Carl
Milles designed the statue, and
legend has it that part of the
statue's forehead comes from
an oak tree that Gustav Vasa
planted himself. The collection
is vast, so it's best if you
choose an area of interest. Are
you into fine china? Lighting
design? Sweden's religious
history? Traditional Indigenous
Sami folk art? Nordiska has
these and more in galleries
on three levels, around a vast
central hall with temporary
exhibits (and a cafe). It's more
storehouse than story, but if
you know what you're looking
for, you'll find it here.

## 5 PRINS EUGENS WALDEMARSUDDE

Prins Eugens väg 6
08 545 837 00
www.waldemarsudde.se
Open Tues–Wed & Fri–Sun
11am–5pm, Thurs 11am–8pm
[MAP p. 152 B4]

It sounds like the kind of place you might write-off as a self-indulgent novelty: the personal museum of the Swedish prince who dabbled in art. But in fact Waldemarsudde, former home and studio of Prince Eugen (1865–1947), puts on eye-opening displays of Nordic painting and sculpture by both emerging and established artists. The crowd skews towards locals engaged in the city's active arts scene; my grandparents visited the place without fail whenever a new exhibition went up. But the main house, gallery and studio make a beautiful backdrop for temporary exhibits as well as items rotated in from the permanent collection. You could also just go for a stroll among the sculptures in the 70,000 square metres of landscaped gardens. I, of course, always start at the museum cafe for coffee and cakes or a shrimp sandwich, and that is a fine approach.

# 6 THIELSKA GALLERIET (THE THIEL GALLERY)

Sjötullsbacken 8
08 662 58 84
www.thielskagalleriet.se
Open Tues–Wed & Fri–Sun
12pm–5pm, Thurs 12pm–8pm
[MAP p. 153 A4]

I tend to be drawn to the dark and gloomy side of Scandinavian art, and this low-key gallery is where I get my fix. Not many visitors make it here – it sits at the far end of Djurgården, meaning either a long walk or a long wait for the infrequent bus #69. I wish more people would visit, because it's a great introduction to some key figures in Scandinavian art – think Edvard Munch (everyone's roommate at university had a poster of his *The Scream*); Carl Larsson (you've probably seen his work, too, he created meticulous illustrations of idyllic Swedish country life); and playwright August Strindberg (*Miss Julie*), whose paintings reflect his stormy soul. Ernest Thiel, a banker and art patron, lived here from 1907 to 1924. Maybe because it was as much a home as a gallery, the space feels intimate and personal. My favourite part is upstairs in the spooky attic, where you'll find Munch's vampire-woman lithographs and, startlingly, philosopher Friedrich Nietzsche's death mask.

# 7 ROSENDALS TRÄDGÅRDSKAFÉ

Rosendalsvägen 38
08 545 812 70
www.rosendalstradgard.se
Open daily 11am–5pm
(Apr–Sept), 11am–4pm
(Oct–Dec & Feb–Mar)
[MAP p. 152 B1]

It would be hard to get fresher food than what you find here as the plant-crowded greenhouse in the heart of this botanical garden grows most of the menu's ingredients. With tables scattered around a herb garden and a kitchen that conjures up biodynamic specials like hearty lamb stew or root-vegetable salad atop (seriously) hyperlocal greens, Rosendals is a dreamy destination for lunch. It makes an ideal goal for a midday stroll around Djurgården, but it's also worth walking or cycling to as a break from the museums on a sunny day. The bakery in an outbuilding next door produces rustic bread, decadent sweet rolls and treats like cheesecake or fruit pie to have with your coffee. In summer you can sit and eat at little tables lined up in the herb garden or scattered around the orchard.

# 8 OAXEN KROG & SLIP

Beckholmsvägen 26
08 551 531 05
oaxen.com
Open daily 12pm–4pm &
5–11pm (Slip); Tues–Sat 6–8pm
(Krog)
[MAP p. 147 E4]

Oaxen consists of two sections inside a corrugated-steel wedge of a building: the Krog is more formal, with two Michelin stars and prices to match; but the Slip bistro is more relaxed and open: tall windows, long tables for communal seating, vintage boats hanging from the ceiling, shareable dishes, and bar seats for drop-in guests. Considering its theme: clean-lined Scandi nautical with vintage details like school desks and old theatre seats, and its location in an old shipyard at the water's edge, it's no surprise that the thing to order here is anything involving fish – especially herring. But the Nordic produce (especially root vegetables and mushrooms) is also outstanding – much of it comes from the meadows of Djurgården – and it's allowed to shine with simple but beautiful presentations. Try the herring with warm potato salad, egg and beetroot, the fish of the day or anything in a berry sauce. In general, you should make reservations. For the best value, hit the Slip for lunch.

# SÖDERMALM

Södermalm has traditionally been the precinct preferred by Stockholm's artists and bohemian types, but that's just one reason so many Stockholmers (not to mention visitors) love it. On the cliffs above Slussen, the locks between this island and Gamla Stan (Old Town), you'll find Bellmansgatan, the namesake street of 18th-century poet and composer Carl Michael Bellman – which, it so happens, is also the address of Mikael Blomkvist, the journalist hero of Stieg Larsson's Millennium trilogy (*Girl with the Dragon Tattoo* et al). As you explore the area, keep an eye out for signs to Monteliusvägen, a tiny footpath that winds its way atop the Söder heights.

Hipster Södermalm's central core is Sofo (South of Folkungagatan), south and east of Medborgarplatsen. Where else can you start with a decadent seafood brunch, then do some record shopping and peruse a bunch of vintage clothing stores, hop into an arcade to play some pinball or shuffleboard, followed by a hefty plate of traditional Swedish meatballs and a beer? Then walk it off along a clifftop path as you watch the fading sunlight play across the black roofs of Gamla Stan.

Tunnelbana: Medborgarplatsen, Slussen, Mariatorget

→ *The view of Gamla Stan and Riddarholmen from Monteliusvägen in the Söder heights*

**SIGHTS**
1. Fotografiska

**SHOPPING**
2. Grandpa
3. Lakritsroten

**SHOPPING & EATING**
4. Urban Deli Nytorget

**EATING**
5. Hermans
6. Mahalo
7. Chutney
8. Pelikan

**DRINKING**
9. Ugglan
10. Kvarnen

# 1 FOTOGRAFI**S**KA

Stadsgårdshamnen 22
08 509 005 00
www.fotografiska.com/sto
Open Sun–Wed 9am–11pm,
Thurs–Sat 9am–1am
[MAP p. 148 C1]

As stylish as it is selective, Fotografiska is a must for anyone interested in photography. The gallery occupies a vast industrial building from 1906 and is a gallery rather than a museum – meaning it's not so much about a permanent collection, although it does have a small one. Fotografiska hosts several temporary exhibitions each year, with work by big names (such as Sebastião Salgado and Irving Penn) as well as emerging artists, including many young artists from Scandinavia. There are usually four major exhibitions per year, plus many more small displays. And don't overlook the short films playing on loop in the tiny screening room; these are often among the most memorable. In summer, an al fresco cafe-bar sets up outside the entrance. Fotografiska's upstairs restaurant is highly rated and often booked, so make reservations.

## 2 GRANDPA

Södermannagatan 21
08 643 6080
www.grandpastore.com
Open Mon–Fri 10am–6.30pm,
Sat 10am–5pm, Sun 11am–
5pm
[MAP p. 148 B3]

**POCKET TIP**
Look for posters
advertising summer
pop-up venues, like
Trädgården, a stage
and bar under a bridge
near Eriksdalsbadet
swimming pool.

Opened by three friends who
wanted to re-create a sense of
what they love about travelling,
Grandpa carries a well-curated
supply of clothing, accessories,
luggage, cool travel gadgets
and coffee table books to
inspire a trip, but there's also
a range of household goods for
nesting when you get home.
I covet the wonky ceramic
mugs by designer Jessica
Hans and the dish sponge
shaped like a fat cat. You can
also find super-stylish office
supplies, cosy woollen scarves
and hats, shoes and boots,
sunglasses, throw blankets and
leather goods. Even if you're
just browsing without intent,
the store has a cool magazine-
styled interior – mid-century
modern furniture, potted
plants, neo-industrial shelves
and lighting – that makes it fun
to wander around in.

GRANDPA
Södermannagatan 21

SALE

# 3 LAKRIT/ROTEN

Hornsgatan 45
08 428 26 08
lakritsroten.se
Open Mon–Fri 10am–6.30pm,
Sat 10am–5pm, Sun
11am–5pm
[MAP p.144 C3]

The Nordic obsession with salted black licorice (lakrits) is a phenomenon. This stylish shop, part of a small chain, sells both salt and sweet licorice in just about every imaginable shape, size and flavour combination, from chocolate or raspberry to violet and lavender, in fetching little tins and packets. The walls are lined with display cases as cute and orderly as what you'd find in a high-end make-up store. If you're not sure you love black licorice as much as the Swedes, here's a handy test: step inside the door and inhale. Good? OK! You're in. There are sections for licorice-based cooking supplies – from licorice powder to big hunks of the raw stuff meant for grating. If you decide you're hooked, go online to reserve a spot at one of the store's regular licorice tastings, sometimes paired with beer or wine.

## 4 URBAN DELI NYTORGET

Nytorget 4
08 425 500 30
www.urbandeli.org
Open Sun–Tues 8am–11pm,
Wed–Thurs 8am–12am, Fri–Sat
8am–1am
[MAP p. 148 C3]

A combination gourmet grocery store and restaurant with outdoor seating in summer, this hopping place draws a beautiful crowd with its stunningly pretty dishes. The weekend brunch is not only delicious but also an entertaining way to see how Stockholmers cope with the after-effects of the city's nightlife. Offerings for the day-after include everything from oysters to waffles, fried eggplant to chilled lobster. Lunch is only marginally simpler; in addition to the regular menu, there are three good-value weekly specials: catch of the day (in a creamy saffron sauce with new potatos) or the vegetable or meat options. Other recommendations include an excellent fiskgryta (fish stew) and a spicy salmon salad with chilli mayo, sesame and cucumbers. Afterwards, pick up some fancy cheeses, cured meats, fresh fruit, wine, olives and crusty homemade bread or packaged salads, soups and prepared meals from the grocery section to take home.

# 5 HERMANS

Fjällgatan 23B
08 643 94 80
www.hermans.se
Open daily 11am–9pm
[MAP p. 148 C1]

Once upon a time, Hermans was a backpacker secret: an all-you-can-eat vegetarian buffet with a low price-tag and a gorgeous setting with water views. Well, Hermans is no longer secret, nor obscenely cheap but the quality and sheer range of dishes make it well worth it. It's usually packed and cheaper at lunchtime, and for dinner you might even want to make a reservation. The setting is as lovely as ever. The buffet room looks like a church nave and you can sit either in an enclosed verandah or outdoors at picnic tables surrounded by trees; some tables have views over the water. Food is made with plant-based ingredients influenced by many cultures. Load up on hearty lasagne, creamy curries, inventive salads and fresh bread, then take your haul to a picnic table in the garden, overlooking the water and the city skyline. Drinks and vegan desserts are also available. Hermans is eco-certified, recycles all waste, and makes work uniforms out of organic cotton.

# 6 MAHALO

Hornsgatan 61
08 420 565 44
www.mahalosthlm.se
Open Mon–Fri 8am–7pm,
Sat–Sun 10am–6pm
[MAP p. 144 B3]

This colourful little cafe is bright and cheery with a fun and vibrant menu of healthy, delicious and filling superfood bowls. The Buddha Bowl is tops, piled high with barbecued tofu, edamame, avocado and other seasonal fresh veggies and herbs on a bed of rice or glass noodles. Try any of the delicious smoothies too. Wait staff are upbeat and helpful with questions, and the space is pretty with an upstairs loft and a long, skinny back patio decorated with colourful flags. The crowd is young and slinky with a healthy glow; on my last visit a guy walked through the place holding a yoga mat. One caveat: don't be in a hurry, as everything is made from scratch and sometimes takes a while.

**POCKET TIP**

Vegan and vegetarian restaurants abound in Södermalm. They're good value and typically offer creative and well-executed dishes with a focus on ultra-fresh, seasonal ingredients.

# 7 CHUTNEY

Katarina Bangata 19
08 640 30 10
www.chutney.se
Open Mon–Fri 11am–10pm, Sat
12pm–10pm, Sun 12pm–9pm
[MAP p. 148 A4]

I bring people to this friendly vegetarian cafe all the time, and it's not because you get a huge amount of really good food for not much money. That's true, but it's not the main reason. Nope: it's the bread. Chutney's meals – which mostly involve massive heaps of vegetarian stews and curries served over rice or potatos – include self-serve bread and salad, and I don't know what they put in the bread but it is like candy: dark, sweet and dense. There's also a case full of lovely-looking desserts but just give me the bread. At the salad station, choose from pitchers of water flavoured with 10 different floating fruits. Or a mix – cucumber–pomegranate, why not? The place is done up in slightly religiously confusing art with an overall vaguely Indian vibe. There's plenty of seating inside and out and very cheerful staff.

## 8 PELIKAN

Blekingegatan 40
08 556 090 90
www.pelikan.se
Open Mon–Tues 4pm–12am,
Wed–Thurs 4pm–1am, Fri–Sun
12pm–1am
[MAP p. 148 A4]

A subdued, grown-up example of the classic Swedish beer hall (which can sometimes have a rowdy party vibe), Pelikan does a fantastic job with traditional husmanskost (Swedish home cooking), particularly the beloved standards, like meatballs (theirs are famously huge) with mashed potatos and lingonberries, fried or pickled herring, cured salmon, or Arctic char (röding). Start with the 'SOS' plate, or 'smör, ost och sill', aka pickled herring with butter, hard bread, cheese and all the toppings. Next-door is an adjoining bar area, recently renovated to look like a glittering modernist jewelbox, serving classic cocktails (martinis, negronis, aviations). In either section, try one of the dozen-plus varieties of aquavit along with your beer; it may be an acquired taste but it's authentically Swedish.

# 9 UGGLAN

Närkesgatan 6
08 641 26 26
ugglanboulebar.se
Open Tues–Thurs 4–11pm,
Fri–Sat 4pm–1am
[MAP p. 148 C4]

The first time my friends brought me to this sprawling, unpretentious bar and arcade, it looked like a bombed-out warehouse: the floor was mostly dirt, the couches were worn and the walls were chipped concrete. I loved it instantly, and I still do, even though it now has a few softer touches such as candlelit tables in one corner. It's large enough that exploring the whole place can be a full evening's adventure. There are bocce courts, shuffleboard, air hockey tables, pinball, and a couple of vintage arcade games (including a rare wall-mounted PacMan machine). Grab a beer at the bar, load your Ugglan card with more credits than you think you'll need and start playing. Note: You have to be at least 23 years old to enter.

**POCKET TIP**
Stockholmers are mad for boules (bocci); look for outdoor courts in most neighbourhood parks, plus boule halls in every precinct.

## 10 KVARNEN

Tjärhovsgatan 4
08 643 03 80
www.kvarnen.com
Open Sun–Tues 4pm–1am,
Wed–Sat 4pm–3am
[MAP p. 148 A2]

A permanent fixture on the Södermalm bar scene, Kvarnen (The Mill) is a traditional, old-fashioned beer hall from 1906 that manages to keep up with the younger crowd without losing its dignity. It was originally a working-class pub but during the 1960s it started to attract some of the neighbourhood's prominent artists, and in the '70s it really took off as the unofficial headquarters of Hammarby football fans – still true today. The main room is an elegant, grown-up space, with tall windows, high ceilings, blonde wood and low lights, perfect for having a dignified pint of Swedish beer and a plate of meatballs, but the late-night scene, when the place becomes a disco, is what it's known for. There's also a cute, steampunk-ish Czech beer bar in the back corner, and a section of outdoor seating around the corner at Medborgarplatsen, Södermalm's main square. Reservations are recommended on weekends and when Hammarby is playing.

**POCKET TIP**

Medborgarplatsen (Citizen Plaza) is Södermalm's busy main square: a meeting place and transit hub lined with food carts and outdoor seating.

# HORNSTULL & LÅNGHOLMEN

Hornstull is part of the large southern island of Södermalm, bounded on three sides by water, and with a low-key vibe that separates it from the ultra-cool, travel-mag-friendly Söder districts like 'SoFo' (South of Folkungagatan). No part of it is touristy. Half of it is Tantolunden park (*see* p. 58), with walking and jogging paths along the edges. It has a diverse population and a public beach where multicultural Swedish families hang out on summer days, watching their kids jump off the diving board. There's a compact knot of shops, bars and restaurants surrounding Hornstull's tunnelbana stop and some of my favourites are here.

Just to the north of Hornstull, connected by two bridges, is the island of Långholmen, which until the 1970s was occupied by a prison (the prison is still here, but now it's a hostel and prison museum). The best way to appreciate this leafy little island is to kayak around it. Långholmen also has two great, sandy swimming beaches, a manicured one called Långholmsbadet behind the hostel and a wilder, more secluded one called Klippbad on the northeast shore. Footpaths go everywhere, some providing gorgeous views across the water to Gamla Stan (Old Town).

Tunnelbana: Hornstull

➻ *Tiny garden cottages in Tantolunden park*

**SIGHTS**
1. Tantolunden
2. Långholmen Kajak

**SHOPPING**
3. Granit

**EATING**
4. Vurma
5. Barbro
6. Lasse i Parken

**DRINK**
7. Hornhuset
8. Bar Brooklyn

# 1 TANTOLUNDEN

Tantolundsvägen
Open daily 24-hrs
[MAP p. 144 A4]

Pack your swimsuit, beach novel and a picnic because this huge greenspace has everything: a swimming and diving beach with a diving board off the dock, wide-open lawns, walking and jogging trails, park benches, miniature golf, volleyball courts, a rock-climbing crag, and two of the open-air gyms that dot the city, with weight-machines made of sturdy logs and wooden planks. What makes this park so special, though, is its community garden. Covering the top of the hill are about 100 garden allotments, each with a heartbreakingly adorable hut or cabin – the kind you want to put in your pocket and take home, and some of them would almost fit! To combat a shortage of produce during World War I, the city allowed working-class families to cultivate garden plots and build huts at Tantolunden. Wander around, pick a favourite and daydream about another life – one where you spend the afternoon sipping coffee in the sun outside a bright red hut with a sky-blue door, surrounded by herbs and flowers. Ahh.

## 2 LÅNGHOLMEN KAJAK

Alstaviksvägen 3
0760 693 852
langholmenkajak.se
Open daily 10am–9pm
(summer), 11am–8pm (May &
Sept)
[MAP p. 157 A1]

**POCKET TIP**

On weekends from
April–Sept, a flea market
(Hornstulls marknad)
spreads out along
Hornstulls Strand at
the water's edge.

Most of Stockholm's prettiest buildings happen to face the water, which means the best way to gaze upon this lovely city is from a kayak. If you hire one from this little dock-stand next to the footbridge between Långholmen and Hornstull, you'll be in the ideal location to start a tour. The system of canals and inlets snaking through the city invites exploration; the water is generally calm and the paddling's easy. Beginners can get some basic instructions before setting out, and staff can recommend routes of various levels that leave from here. The standard route is a loop around Kungsholmen, but shorter or longer trips are also possible. The place offers well-maintained one- and two-person sea kayaks as well as stand-up paddleboards (SUP). If you're nervous about setting out on your own, you can also book a guided trip.

## 3 GRANIT

36 Långholmsgatan
08 462 66 83
www.granit.com
Open Mon–Fri 10am–7pm,
Sat 10am–5pm, Sun 12pm–5pm
[MAP p. 157 C3]

The Swedes are renowned for making ordinary objects look beautiful, and if you're looking for authentic Scandinavian homewares, here is an affordable and accessible design store. Granit is your one-stop shop for household goods and gadgets, with a few locations around town. It's fun to shop here, partly because Swedish people shop here – the products are used in the homes of ordinary Swedes. So go ahead and pick up that authentic Swedish dish towel, pillowcase or throw blanket, that cute storage basket or recipe box. Plenty to fill your suitcase with! When someone asks you if you got it from IKEA (not that there's anything wrong with that), you can say it came from a neighbourhood shop full of locals.

## 4 VURMA

Bergsunds strand 31
08 669 09 60
www.vurma.se
Open daily 9am–7pm
[MAP p. 157 B3]

It's rare that I get a fierce craving for things like kale and beetroot, but when it happens, I seek out Vurma, a neighbourhood cafe (with locations in a few different neighbourhoods). It's less interested in superfoods than in making substantial, satisfying meals, whether it's a salad, a sandwich or a healthy bowl of greens and grains. Menu offerings change, but a recent favourite was roasted chicken with lime, spicy sauce, pepitas and tons of fresh veggies over red quinoa. Or try the vegan falafel salad or the grilled prosciutto sandwich with chevre, mango and mint. There are lots of creative vegan and vegetarian options, usually with Asian- or Mediterranean-leaning ingredients (such as buckwheat noodles, couscous and halloumi cheese). The chairs are decorated with brightly coloured cushions and the tiny tables are set close together, creating opportunities to chat with a neighbour if you're so inclined. And since lunch was so nutritious, you should probably also get a homemade brownie or cinnamon bun.

## 5 BARBRO

Hornstulls strand 13
08 550 602 66
bar-bro.se
Open Tues–Thurs 5–11pm,
Fri–Sat 5pm–12.30am, Sun
5–9pm
[MAP p. 157 C4]

At first glance, Barbro looks like a sleek, minimalist Asian-fusion restaurant – all sharp angles, straight lines and neo-industrial lighting fixtures, serving unusual, creative takes on sushi and sashimi – but it's also a cinema (more on that soon). Dine on duck-liver wontons, beef sashimi, dumplings spiced with coriander and chilli, as well as the excellent cocktail list. Try the tart yuzu margarita (yuzu is an Asian citrus fruit), the Ume-shu Sour (made with Japanese plum wine) or the Gingerdoll, with bourbon, lemon and fresh ginger. The bar downstairs doubles as 'Salong 4', a screening room that shows international films and new releases, plus live music and, occasionally, football matches. So your dinner and a movie can include a spicy tuna roll and an Old Fashioned while you watch. Reservations are recommended but if you're just one or two, you can often squeeze in at the bar.

### POCKET TIP
For a stroll through Swedish drinking history, cross the tiny bridge from Hornstull to Reimersholme, original location of Absolut vodka's distillery.

UNDER BARB

# 6 LASSE I PARKEN

Högalidsgatan 56
08 658 33 95
www.lasseiparken.se
Open Mon–Sat 11am–10pm,
Sun 11am–5pm (Apr–Sept), by
reservation in Dec
[MAP p. 157 B2]

Relax and enjoy your afternoon coffee or after-work beer among the little covered tables and lush greenery in this cafe that feels more like a garden. Most of the seating is outdoors (much of it covered by patio roofs), in a fenced yard filled with potted plants and flowering shrubs. It's the sort of place your imaginary Swedish cousin who lives out in the country might invite you to for brunch or high tea. The main building is a 17th-century red-painted wooden Swedish farmhouse with a red picket fence surrounding the grounds. There's a stage for outdoor concerts in summer. The cafe menu is mostly salads and sandwiches (the shrimp sandwich is always a good choice); in the evening, there's a brief menu of Swedish favourites like röding (Arctic char) or Wallenburgare (a ground veal patty usually served with mashed potatos and green peas).

## 7 HORNHUSET

Långholmsgatan 15B
08 525 202 60
www.hornhuset.se
Opening hours vary
[MAP p. 157 C3]

Hornhuset, a multi-tiered bar and nightclub that sits above the Hornstull tunnelbana (train) stop, looks a bit like a stack of boxes that someone bumped into, nudging it sideways. Its four levels each have their own names, themes, and hours. The summer-only rooftop bar, **Barrio**, is the best, with its lofty views over several residential blocks, canals and inlets, and its fairy lights and bright-pink and -yellow chairs. On the ground floor is a Peruvian-style ceviche and taco bar called **Barranco**, a popular spot for after-work drinks – try a pisco sour, or a Cori Collins, with gin and coriander. Above that is **Laika**, a sleek nightclub with DJs and dancing, and above that, somewhat incongruously, is **Enzo's**, a casual Italian trattoria serving handmade pizza to enthusiastic football fans. They're all open late (until 1 or 3am) on Friday and Saturday nights.

### POCKET TIP

The Hornstull tunnelbana station's shopping centre contains a huge supermarket, bakery, sushi restaurant, coffee shop and chain stores like Sweden's H&M.

## 8 BAR BROOKLYN

Honstrulls strand 4
08 658 63 50
debaser.se/barbrooklyn
Open Fri–Sat 6pm–3am & most
weeknights for events; Wed–Sat
6pm–late (Jun–Aug)
[MAP p. 157 C4]

A dimly lit, casual bar along the water's edge, Bar Brooklyn is part of the adjoining Debaser music venue (which includes a Mexican restaurant) and is a wonderfully intimate place to see a live show. It's also a comfortable, unfussy spot for just a burger and a beer (or a milkshake!) in the evenings, with lots of small nooks where you can settle into a comfy chair or leather sofa. The bar has ties to Brooklyn Brewery in New York, and its tap list is weighted heavily toward the American craft-brew scene (especially the serviceable but unexciting Brooklyn Lager). There's a good cocktail menu, with reliable standards like the Old Fashioned alongside seasonal specialties like pomegranate margaritas, plus shuffleboard, quiz nights and stand-up comedy (I watched some World Cup football matches here). In summer, the bar has nice tables for outdoor seating – great for watching the foot traffic along the waterfront.

# ÖSTERMALM

Long established as the wealthiest part of town, Östermalm is also a party zone. Its elegant, dignified streets, lined with palatial residential buildings and luxury retail shops, are also where you'll find the city's more famous nightclubs. As such, it's a delight to wander day or night, whether the eye candy you prefer is architectural or fashion-oriented. If you have a secret Swedish celebrity crush keep your eyes peeled, as this is the area where you'll have the best chance of a sighting. At the centre of the precinct, you'll find a public square (actually more of a triangle) called Stureplan, marked by a modernist concrete pavilion called Svampen ('the mushroom', reflecting its shape), a favourite meeting point for people going out on the town. People-watching around Svampen provides a quick tutorial in what to wear for a night out at Stockholm clubs.

Östermalm is also home to the Swedish history museum, Historiska Museet (see p. 70) and the pleasant green park called Humlegården, populated by a mixture of students hitting the books and former supermodel parents pushing baby strollers.

Tunnelbana: Östermalmstorg; ferry lines: Nybrokajen, Strandvägen

→ *Wild floral prints are a specialty at Svenskt Tenn*

### SIGHTS
1. Historiska Museet (Swedish History Museum)
2. Dramaten (Royal Dramatic Theatre)

### SHOPPING
3. Svenskt Tenn
4. Hedengrens

### SHOPPING & EATING
5. Östermalms Saluhall

### EATING
6. Sturekatten
7. Sturehof

# 1 HISTORISKA MUSEET (SWEDISH HISTORY MUSEUM)

Narvavägen 13-17
08 519 556 00
historiska.se
Open Tues–Sun 11am–5pm,
Wed 11am–8pm
[MAP p. 149 B1]

With its moody, blue-lit halls and glittering display cases of battered helmets, ancient swords and jewellery, this history museum strikes the perfect balance of insight and mystery. Have you ever wondered who the Vikings were really? How much can we really know about the past? Does it matter which people are doing the recording? Which isn't to say the museum is heavy or grim – the Viking exhibit is enthralling, for kids and adults in equal measure. There's a story corner where you can learn about the Norse gods, and a place where kids can practice their archaeological digging, plus an outdoor section with a labyrinth and model ship. Don't miss the Gold Room, with its rune-inscribed entryway. Upstairs there's a walk-through display that leads you through the decades, from displays on medieval royalty and early peasant life to modern Swedish kitchens and immigration policies. It is as close as you can get to stepping onto the pages of a history book.

## 2 DRAMATEN (ROYAL DRAMATIC THEATRE)

Nybroplan
08 667 06 80
www.dramaten.se
Open for tours and
performances
[MAP p. 143 E3]

One of the cutest buildings in
Stockholm, the Royal Dramatic
Theatre is so well-loved it even
has a nickname – Dramaten
means The Drama. There
are four stages in the squat
marble building, built in 1908.
Iconic Swedish filmmaker
Ingmar Bergman (*Persona*,
*The Seventh Seal*) worked
here for 40 years and swore
he would return to haunt it
after his death – this can be
neither confirmed nor denied.
Performances generally take
place in Swedish, but English
speakers can still enjoy it or
sign up for one of the theatre's
one-hour guided tours instead
(Saturdays at 5pm, more
frequently during the summer
season). The tours take you
behind the scenes to see
costumes and sets from early
Bergman plays, and discuss
the artwork that decorates the
theatre's interior (Dramaten
owns many pieces by well-
known Scandinavian artists)
and the building's design.

**POCKET TIP**

The statue outside
Dramaten is Swedish
actress Margaret Krook;
touch her belly for
luck – it's kept
heated to 37°C.

# 3 SVENSKT TENN

Strandvägen 5
08 670 16 00
www.svenskttenn.se
Open Mon–Fri 10am–6.30pm,
Sat 10am–5pm, Sun
11am–4pm
[MAP p. 143 F3]

For a fast and thorough
tutorial in Swedish interior
design, take a stroll through
the spaces at this venerable
shop – the envy of every
design blog. Dominating
Stockholm's design world since
the early 1930s, this shop –
established by pewter artists
whose interests later shifted
towards interior design – is
immediately recognisable.
Its aesthetic was shaped by
founder Estrid Ericson and the
Austrian artist Josef Frank, a
key figure in the Vienna School
of Architecture, who with his
Swedish wife fled to Stockholm
in 1934 to escape Nazism.
Frank's signature patterns –
wildly colourful, splashy, lively
scenes of floral chaos – cover
everything from chairs and
sofas (which Frank also
designed) to rugs and window
dressings to much more
affordable paper napkins and
serving trays which make ideal
gifts. The little vignettes set up
in each nook of the store prove
that there's really no such thing
as clashing patterns. Upstairs
is a tea room where you can
have a light meal in a perfectly
curated space.

**POCKET TIP**

Pretty Strandvägen is a waterfront street lined with stately mansions, along which the gloomy Swedish writer and artist August Strindberg used to pace and ponder.

## 4 HEDENGRENS

Stureplan 4, Sturegallerian
08 611 46 06
www.hedengrens.se
Open Mon–Fri 10am–7pm, Sat
10am–5pm, Sun 12pm–5pm
[MAP p. 143 D1]

Bibliophiles, especially those who read English and French, should rush directly to Hedengrens, the long-established independent bookstore inside posh shopping centre Sturegallerian. Started in 1897, Hedengrens has a welcoming, helpful staff and a large section of books in English and other foreign languages, including popular Swedish writers in translation. The stock in English goes well beyond the usual top 10 bestsellers. There are books of literary fiction, science fiction and fantasy, art and photography, science, nature and popular non-fiction, most in multiple languages. Head downstairs to the lower level for the widest selection – this is also where the store holds author readings and book signings (schedules online), with both Swedish and international authors. Be sure to check out the cylindrical book room on the lower level, then peek into it from the ground floor.

**POCKET TIP**
In Sturegallerian you'll find high-end men's and women's fashion, plus a day spa and several upscale cafes, bars and restaurants.

# 5 ÖSTERMALMS SALUHALL

Östermalmstorg 14
www.ostermalmshallen.se
Open Mon–Fri 9.30am–7pm,
Sat 9.30am–5pm
[MAP p. 143 F1]

This high-end food market is your go-to in Stockholm for luxury picnic supplies befitting this upscale neighbourhood. There's reindeer sausage, specialty cheeses from various regions in Sweden, artisan breads and locally grown Swedish produce, from strawberries to mushrooms. I can't decide whether to recommend that you 'show up hungry' or 'definitely do not show up hungry'. Either way, you'll want to eat everything you see here. Though it's in new digs until at least mid-2019 while its original home in a historic market hall is being renovated, on the inside it feels the same as ever. Wander the aisles and gaze upon endless display cases of prepared foods (such as smoked salmon, salads, pickled herring, sandwiches, lasagna, quiche and gratin), fresh produce, just-caught seafood, cured meats, bread, sweets, coffee, tea, spices, chocolates and fancy cheeses. Mixed in with all of that are a handful of top-notch restaurants, notably seafood favourites **Tysta Mari** and **Lisa Elmqvist**. So, yes, it's probably best to arrive hungry.

# 6 STUREKATTEN

Riddargatan 4
08 611 16 12
www.sturekatten.se
Open Mon–Fri 9am–7pm, Sat
9am–6pm, Sun 10am–6pm
[MAP p. 143 E2]

This sweet, old-fashioned
coffeehouse has a look that
will be catnip to anyone with
a case of Old World nostalgia
with its antique furniture,
lace curtains and faded
paintings – plus a display
case of tempting cakes and
pastries and an adorable
outdoor courtyard with extra
seating in warm weather. It's
inside a two-storey apartment
building; you walk up a
creaky, winding staircase to
get in. Sandwiches, salads
and hot meals are available
here too, but it's hard to
resist going straight for coffee
and dessert. Try a princess
cake (prinsesstårta), the
Swedish classic of pillowy
green marzipan and sponge
cake, or a big slice of fruit pie
covered in cream.

# 7 STUREHOF

Stureplan 2
08 440 57 30
www.sturehof.com
Open daily 11am–2am
[MAP p. 143 D1]

Exemplifying the spirit and style of Östermalm, Sturehof is a fabulous seafood restaurant that is at least as much about being seen as being sated. If you can, get a table on the outdoor terrace, where the street-level location makes it easy to observe the habits of Stockholm's most stylish inhabitants. In addition to this premium seating at simple outdoor tables, there's a tiny, bright, white-tiled standing bar; a large, airy, gold-trimmed modern dining room; a private room at the back with hanging lamps in cute red ballerina dresses; and a sleek black-walled cocktail bar that's open late. Sometimes yet another bar pops up in the atrium of the adjoining Sturegallerian shopping centre. The menu is huge and changes daily, depending on the day's catch, but you can't really go wrong; if in doubt, start with pickled herring (three or five types, with fixings) and then ask for seasonal recommendations. I recommend any dish involving poached cod or steamed Arctic char (röding), but you could also splash out on a plate of oysters or half a lobster.

**POCKET TIP**
Östermalm's hottest nightclub varies week to week, so ask around. They get hopping around midnight and close at 4 or 5am.

77

# VASASTAN

Just far enough from the city centre to feel like an insiders secret, yet easy to reach on foot or public transport, this precinct holds special appeal to visitors who want to immerse themselves in local life. It's mostly residential, with small shops and a range of well-loved, unpretentious restaurants dotting its quiet, leafy streets. Unlike with most of Stockholm's precincts, it's not always clear when you've arrived in Vasastan; there's no obvious border or body of water separating it from the urban core of Norrmalm or the shiny streets of Östermalm. More or less, Vasastan's boundaries are roughly Birger Jarlsgatan to the east, Tegnérgatan to the south, the train tracks and Klarastrandsleden to the west, and the E20 motorway to the north. But for practical purposes, I usually think of it as the precinct that radiates out from the busy Odenplan transit hub.

A great place to observe the locals in their natural habitat is the very pretty Vasaparken (Vasa Park, *see* p. 81), which makes a wonderful introduction to this friendly precinct.

Tunnelbana: Odenplan, Rådmansgatan

↪ *Odenplan is a busy transit hub at the heart of Vasastan*

**SIGHTS**
1. Stadsbiblioteket
   (Stockholm Public Library)
2. Strindbergsmuseet
   (Strindberg Museum)

**SHOPPING**
3. Nostalgipalatset
4. Myrorna

5. Acne Archive

**EATING**
6. Flippin' Burgers
7. Tranan
8. Tennstopet

# 1 ſTADſBIBLIOTEKET (ſTOCKHOLM PUBLIC LIBRARY)

Sveavägen 73
08 508 31 100
biblioteket.stockholm.se
Open Mon–Thurs 10am–9pm,
Fri 10am–7pm, Sat–Sun
11am–5pm
[MAP p. 155 F1]

The main branch of Stockholm's public library system, Stadsbiblioteket contains around two million volumes, plus audio and video recordings. Opened in 1928, it was designed by famed Swedish architect Gunnar Asplund, whose plans included the little park to the south of the library and the block of storefronts just below the building along Sveavägen. Even the untrained eye can appreciate the structure's beauty and the simplicity of its design, sometimes called Swedish Grace. To complete the experience, go inside and get a sense of how that cylindrical atrium works when it's lined with endless rows of books. It was one of the first in Sweden to allow direct access to bookshelves, so readers could browse and handpick books. And while you're here, the library is also a handy place to catch up on your travel blog or get a little work done.

## POCKET TIP

Vasaparken is a favourite spot for picnic lunches, study breaks, after-work hangouts, and play dates with the kids (its playground has brand-new facilities).

# 2 STRINDBERGSMUSEET (STRINDBERG MUSEUM)

Drottninggatan 85
08 441 91 70
www.strindbergsmuseet.se
Open Tues–Sun 12pm–4pm
[MAP p. 155 F4]

The notoriously tempestuous author, painter and playwright August Strindberg (1849–1912) lived and worked in the building he called the Blue Tower for the last four years of his life. The building is noticeably not blue – it got its nickname because in Strindberg's day, the staircase walls were blue. The rooms he occupied have been preserved as a museum and archive; you can see his desk, bedroom and kitchen as they looked when he lived there. His writing employed naturalism and symbolism to lash out against social conventions and accepted patterns of thought; he basically invented modern Swedish drama, but the intensity of his work (and his turbulent romantic life) wreaked havoc on his mental health. Strindberg's work and life were tightly intertwined – he meticulously described his real-world surroundings in many works, notably *The Red Room* (1879) – so it's a treat to see his rooms in person. Accompanying text, photos and letters place the author's often provocative ideas in their social context.

**POCKET TIP**

After your visit, walk a block west to Tegnérlunden Park and see the sculpture of a tormented Strindberg by beloved Swedish artist Carl Eldh.

# 3 NOSTALGIPALATSET

Sankt Eriksgatan 101
08 34 00 61
www.nostalgipalatset.com
Open Mon–Fri 11am–7pm,
Sat 11am–4pm
[MAP p. 154 A1]

If you're a collector or admirer of pop-culture, this store is bound to get your pulse racing. It's a big shop crammed full of vinyl records, vintage toys, movie posters, and other collectibles and memorabilia. Plan to spend some time digging through the crates of records – you might get lucky and find a treasure in the New Arrivals section, or this could be your chance to pick up some music by Swedish bands that might be hard to find back home. A fun thing to do is flip through the covers of Swedish dance band albums and marvel at the hair-and-wardrobe choices. You can also find treasures like autographed press photos of ABBA, the full line-up of *Star Wars* figures in protective casings, tiny race cars still in their boxes and vintage pop-culture magazines.

## 4 MYRORNA

Norrtullsgatan 9
08 34 82 20
www.myrorna.se
Open Mon–Fri 10am–6pm,
Sat 10am–4pm
[MAP p.155 E2]

Retail shopping in Stockholm is not always cheap but luckily second-hand stores and thrift shops are excellent places to stumble upon budget treasures. Myrorna is one of a handful of second-hand chains with several locations around the city. Its stock is well organised and selectively curated, and there's a fairly high turnover, so your chances of scoring a classic Acne (see p. 86) denim jacket or vintage dress are good. As always with thrifting, it's a treasure hunt, but you might find a vintage Diane von Furstenburg wrap dress or a Tiger of Sweden blazer hidden among the even-cheaper-than-retail H&M skirts and tops. I've stumbled across exclusive Swedish designer brands like House of Dagmar just hanging there next to a pair of old Levi's. The shop also carries household goods, and you can often find high-end glassware and china – say, an iconic Stig Lindberg blue-plum coffee mug or a delicate Kosta Boda vase – that would cost the earth if you bought them brand-new.

**POCKET TIP**

Need a snack while shopping? Head to Günthers (Karlbergsvägen 66), a gourmet sausage stand with over 20 kinds of hotdog.

## 5 ACNE ARCHIVE

Torsgatan 53
08 302 723
www.acnestudios.com/stores/
torsgatan
Open Mon–Fri 11am–6.30pm,
Sat 11am–5.30pm, Sun
12pm–5pm
[MAP p.154 A2]

Almost as much a gallery as
a store, this tiny, sparsely
decorated outlet of the famous
Swedish men's and women's
clothing brand (originally
known for its denim) is where
to find both exclusive pieces,
one-of-a-kind items from
previous collections, and
classics whose prices have
been wildly marked down. Of
course, it's still Acne, a high-
end Swedish designer clothing
brand, so don't expect bargain-
basement prices – but if you're
looking for an excuse to invest
in some high-quality denim or
even splurge on a big-ticket
item that you can't get at home
(such as parkas, dresses), this
is the place. The brand has
several other shops around
Stockholm, but the Archive is
where the best deals live.

## 6 FLIPPIN' BURGER*∫*

Observatoriegatan 8
flippinburgers.se
Open Mon–Thurs 4–10pm,
Fri 11am–10pm, Sat–Sun
12pm–10pm
[MAP p. 155 E3]

This American-style diner would be massively popular even if it didn't serve some of the best burgers in town, just because it's such a fun place: good music, '50s decor, knick-knacks everywhere. The burgers are made with hand-shaped patties and free-range beef ground daily in-house, on organic buns, with just the basic toppings – lettuce, cheese, tomato and onion. You can also get a milkshake with a shot of Jack Daniels in it – like an adult! The restaurant doesn't take reservations, and it's always busy, so you'll most likely have to wait a bit for a table unless you show up the minute they open on a weekday, or during the lull around 3pm on weekends.

# 7 TRANAN

Karlbergsvägen 14
08 527 281 00
www.tranan.se
Open Mon–Fri 11.30am–11pm,
Sat–Sun 12pm–11pm
[MAP p. 155 D1]

A beloved neighbourhood restaurant, Tranan is known for gorgeous classic Swedish dishes in an elegant setting that somehow also feels relaxed and casual: think fine china and candles on red-checked tablecloths, and sharply dressed staff in vests and ties. Specialties include Swedish meatballs (not always on the menu, but ask as it's always available) and fried herring, a house specialty since the restaurant's earliest days – it opened in 1929. Back then Tranan was an occasionally rowdy beer hall – the kind of place that wasn't allowed to have its curtains closed, by order of the police. Clientele were builders and other workmen (pretty much exclusively men). Reached by a separate entrance to the right of the main cafe, the cellar was originally a place for fine dining; these days, it's a dance club that opens late at night, with frequent live music.

# 8 TENNSTOPET

Dalagatan 50
08 32 25 18
www.tennstopet.se
Open Mon–Fri 11.30am–1pm,
Sat–Sun 1am–1pm
[MAP p. 154 C2]

Another longstanding neighbourhood favourite, Tennstopet serves meals you *could* probably make at home, but they wouldn't be anywhere near as tasty. Best example: pytt i panna, which is essentially 'Swedish hash' – chopped potatos and meat and whatever else is leftover all fried in a pan, served with a fried egg and red beets. Tennstopet's version of 'SOS' – smör, ost och sill, or butter, cheese and herring – is also a winner, as is the cured salmon plate, with potatos in dill sauce. The main room looks like a Swedish interpretation of a Scottish pub, with red tartan carpet and wall coverings, a long wooden bar, a carved wooden ceiling and an elk head over the doorway. Off to the side is a more refined, elegant dining room, all chandeliers and ceramic tiles. It's a local's hangout, and staff are open and friendly. If you belly up to the bar and chat while you eat, you're bound to make friends and learn something about Stockholm you didn't know before.

# LADUGÅRDſGÄRDET

Locally known as Gärdet, this mostly residential precinct includes part of Stockholm's National City Park, a network linking several massive green spaces throughout the city. The centrepiece is a wide-open, mostly flat, grassy sports field, historically used as pastureland for the royal family's livestock. Later it became shared public grazing land, and then in the late 1600s a venue for military demonstrations, war games and royal parades, as well as a training ground for new recruits. King Karl XIV Johan had a small pavilion built overlooking the fields, a cute pink building that, despite its name ('Royal Fortress'), looks decidedly un-fortresslike. Today the enormous sports field contains volleyball courts, soccer pitches, cycling and walking paths, and enough open space to hold all manner of events, from American football games to horse races.

In addition to being a fantastic place for a long walk or a jog on a nice day, Gärdet is home to three great museums gathered at the edge of its main field: the National Museum of Science and Technology (see p.92), the Museum of Ethnography (see p. 93) and the Maritime Museum (see p. 94). It's also a good place to get a quick sense of trends in modern Swedish residential architecture; most of the buildings here are apartments designed in the '30s as a sort of high-urban-density utopia aimed at providing all the modern comforts while being well integrated into the natural environment. The latest example of this effort is the striking apartment complex 79&Park (see p. 93).

Bus: 68, 69 (Museiparken), 72, 76 (Filmhuset)

Tunnelbana: Gärdet, Karlaplan

→ Filmhuset, home of the Swedish Film Institute

**FILMHUSET**

**SKA FILMINSTITUTET**

**AFER BAR & RESTAURANG**

**SIGHTS**
1. Tekniska Museet (National Museum of Science and Technology)
2. Etnografiska Museet (Museum of Ethnography)
3. Sjöhistoriska Museet (Maritime Museum)
4. Filmhuset (The Film House)
5. Kaknästornet

**EATING**
6. Djurgårdsbrunn
7. Carotte

# 1 TEKNIJKA MUJEET (NATIONAL MUJEUM OF JCIENCE AND TECHNOLOGY)

Museivägen 7
08 450 56 00
www.tekniskamuseet.se
Open Tues & Thurs–Fri
10am–5pm, Wed 10am–8pm
[MAP p. 151 D4]

Bring your children or offer to babysit someone else's if it makes you feel better, but don't let the fact that you're a full-grown adult stop you from having fun at this interactive science and technology museum. You might even learn something! The larger-than-life puzzles begin before you even get in the door, in the Mathematical Garden, with mazes, slides and games designed to make numbers fun. Inside, exhibits change periodically but cover topics like virtual reality, cosplay (you can be Darth Vader for a day!), interstellar travel, kinetic energy, robots and home computer systems. Most exhibits focus on the intersection of technology, design, and daily life. The gift shop has puzzles, toys, books and games geared towards teaching scientific concepts.

**POCKET TIP**

Take a peek at 79&Park's multi-tiered green-roof terraces and pixellated facade, designed by Scandinavian 'starchitect' firm the BIG Group.

## 2 ETNOGRAFISKA MUSEET (MUSEUM OF ETHNOGRAPHY)

Djugårdsbrunnsvägen 34
010 456 12 00
www.varldskulturmuseerna.se/
en/etnografiskamuseet/
Open Tues & Thurs–Sun
11am–5pm, Wed 11am–8pm
[MAP p.151 D4]

One of the more ambitious and well-executed museums in Stockholm, Etnografiska looks at both ancient and modern cultures with a steadfastly neutral, curious gaze. In different corners of the museum, visitors might learn about, say, a Japanese tea ceremony, a Native American teepee, tools from early Indigenous Sami life, or ceremonial dance masks from parts of Africa. Temporary exhibits sometimes aim closer to home: a recent one tackled body image across various contemporary societies. A glass-windowed wonder cabinet occupies one hall, its 6,000 items stored in apparent disorder, adding a sense of discovery as you wander. Most of the displays incorporate video, sound, light and other multimedia components. The attached restaurant, **Matmekka**, serves an organic pan-Asian lunch buffet, a wide range of desserts and a good children's menu.

# 3 SJÖHISTORISKA MUSEET (MARITIME MUSEUM)

Djurgårdsbrunnsvägen 24
08 519 549 00
www.sjohistoriska.se/en
Open Tues–Sun 10am–5pm
[MAP p. 150 C4]

Stockholm – a city built on a series of islands – has a history that depends heavily on maritime history, so much so that a museum about one can hardly help including the other. The maritime museum, in a wonderful crescent-shaped building designed for the purpose, displays about 2,000 different model ships, but also gets into the region's naval history and the development of commercial shipping from the earliest days of the Hanseatic League (started in the 1300s). Some of the model ships are truly amazing to see (no touching!), with fully operational steam engines, doors that lock, miniature sails that actually hoist via accurately to-scale cables. There's even white tablecloths on the dining room tables and pillows on the cabin beds in the cruise-ship models. The museum houses a huge photographic and archive collection, a fascinating collection of figureheads from old vessels, and many temporary exhibitions.

## 4 FILMHUSET (THE FILM HOUSE)

Borgvägen 1-5
08 665 11 00
www.filminstitutet.se/Filmhuset
Open for screenings
Tues–Sun; library open Mon–Fri
11am–4pm
[MAP p. 150 A1]

It seems appropriate that a building dedicated to film would itself be visually striking. The Swedish Film Institute has been screening and archiving film since the 1960s and Filmhuset, the Film House, its dedicated venue, opened in 1971. The entryway is designed to look like a strip of film with sprocket holes and from above, the building is supposed to look like a camera. There's a great library of film stills and posters you can look through, plus a massive collection of books and magazines related to international film culture. Screenings are curated by Cinemateket, a film education organisation that brings foreign and domestic masterpieces, new talents and obscure art films to a wider audience. Films are often presented by the director or star with a Q&A; check schedules online. The bar and bistro serves an organic, buffet lunch from 11am to 2pm weekdays.

95

LADUGÅRDSGÄRDET

# 5 KAKNÄSTORNET

Mörka kroken 28–30
08 667 21 80
www.kaknastornet.se
Open daily 10am–6pm,
longer hours in summer and
some weekends
[MAP p. 151 E3]

I'll admit that I risk having a
panic attack every time I visit
this place but it's worth it. The
long, cramped elevator ride to
the 30th-floor observation deck
is not for the faint of heart,
and it's no better coming back
down. But the 360-degree
views from here, a 155-metre-
high TV tower built in 1967
and still in use, are impressive.
The tower is also really handy
as a landmark. There's an
outdoor observation platform
at the top, as well as a cafe
serving sandwiches, cakes
and coffee (and an overpriced,
reservations-only restaurant)
with equally good views. On a
clear day, you can see for miles
in every direction, even the
nearer islands of the Stockholm
archipelago (see p. 112). It's
fun to search out places you've
visited, pinpoint the street
where your hotel is, or just get
a new appreciation of the city's
layout. It's also a nice place
to watch the sun set. If the
weather's not clear, save it for
another day.

## 6 DJURGÅRD/BRUNN

Djurgårdsbrunnsvägen 68
08 624 22 00
djurgardsbrunn.com
Open Wed–Thurs 5–10pm,
Fri 5–11pm, Sat 11.30am–4pm
& 5.30–11.30pm, Sun
11.30am–4pm
[MAP p. 151 F4]

On a hill beside the canal
(Djurgårdsbrunnskanalen)
that runs between Gärdet and
Djurgården, and best reached
by the canalside footpath,
this cheerful restaurant has
a deceptively beachy vibe in
summer, with lawn chairs for
outdoor seating, a table in
a cute yellow pagoda, wide
grassy lawns and three boules/
bocce courts. Indoors, however,
the (year-round) restaurant
is formal and elegant, with
fixed-price dinner menus of
French- and Mediterranean-
accented Swedish standards
(chanterelle soup with
pumpkin risotto, steamed cod
with root vegetables), and a
fancy brunch on the weekends
(such as smoked salmon,
cheesecake, Spanish omelette).
Brunch is definitely your best
bet; plan on a morning of
wandering the trails through
the fields and woods of Gärdet,
then follow the canal back here
and settle into a lazy weekend.

**POCKET TIP**
For a less elaborate
morning coffee, follow
the canal path east past
Gärdet to Kafé Kruthuset
for pastries and simple
sandwiches.

## 7 CAROTTE

Tegeluddsvägen 92
08 655 11 22
carotte.se
Open Mon–Fri 7.30am–3pm
[MAP p. 150 C1]

The Frihamnen location (at the edge of Gärdet) of this deli/catering kitchen fills a serious gap in the line-up of places to get a healthy midday meal in this precinct; it's great if you want to pick up picnic supplies before a walk through the park. The deli occupies a cool, shiny industrial space with high ceilings, huge windows and whitewashed brick walls. Its display cases show off vividly nutritious-looking dishes, smoothies and freshly squeezed juices in bright jewel-tones of orange, green and red. You can probably get your recommended daily amount of Vitamin C just walking in and looking at the menu. (But don't worry, there are also decadent pastries and sweet rolls. Life is balance.) Menus change weekly, but I like the sesame-coated salmon with veggies and the falafel plate.

# KUNGSHOLMEN

Kungsholmen is a residential neighbourhood in the truest sense – apart from the major draw of Stadshuset (City Hall *see* p. 102) at its inner edge, the pleasures of Kungsholmen include ordinary Stockholm everyday experiences, like admiring docked boats as you stroll along the waterfront on wide, tree-lined Norr Mälarstrand, gazing across the water at the steeples and palaces of Riddarholmen and the Gamla Stan (Old Town) skyline. Or wandering up and down quiet residential streets lined with stately apartment buildings and dotted with parks, supermarkets, banks, thrift shops, sushi joints and lighting stores – typical streets like Hantverkargatan or Sankt Eriksgatan, which funnel you in toward busy Fridhemsplan, a lively commercial hub well-connected to the city centre and outlying neighbourhoods by public transport.

Another highlight is hanging out in Rålambshovsparken (*see* p. 103), one of the city's biggest parks, whether joining the early birds for a workout at the outdoor gym, taking the kids to the playground or going for an afternoon jog along the network of dedicated footpaths. In short, it's the kind of precinct where you can imagine what it would feel like to live in Stockholm.

Tunnelbana: Rådhuset, Fridhemsplan; bus 3 (Fleminggatan, Stadshuset)

→ *Skatepark at Rålambshovs Parken*

**SIGHTS**
1. Stadshuset (City Hall)
2. Rålambshovs Parken

**SHOPPING**
3. Naturkompaniet

**SHOPPING & EATING**
4. Västermalms Gallerian

**EATING & DRINKING**
5. Phil's Burger
6. Mälarpaviljongen
7. Biljardpalatset

# 1 STADSHUSET (CITY HALL)

Hantverkargatan 1
08 508 290 58
www.stockholm.se/
OmStockholm/Stadshuset
Open by guided tour
[MAP p. 144 B1]

You don't have to win a Nobel Prize to get a peek at the fabulous Blue Hall where the annual Nobel banquet is held – you can just take a tour. The hall is inside Stockholm's City Hall, one of the city's most architecturally distinctive buildings (designed by noted Swedish architect Ragnar Östberg), also known for the terraces on which locals sunbathe on hot summer days. The catch: City Hall can only be visited on a guided tour as the building is full of offices and people working might find gawkers disruptive. On a tour you'll descend the wide marble staircase into the Blue Hall, and learn about the patterned floor, the colonnaded brick hall, and the immense effort to pull off a formal dinner for 1,400 distinguished guests. You'll also see the spectacular Golden Hall, a banquet room with glittering mosaics decorating its walls, in which 18 million tiles show scenes from Swedish history. There are usually six daily tours in English; check schedules online, you can't buy tickets in advance.

**POCKET TIP**
For amazing views, climb to the top of the 106-metre-high tower, open daily May–September. An elevator goes about halfway up.

## 2 RÅLAMBSHOVS PARKEN

Smedsuddsvägen 6
08 618 62 91
Open daily 24-hrs
[MAP p. 156 A3]

If I lived anywhere near this beautiful green waterfront park, I think I might actually follow through on all of my fitness aspirations. The place *begs* you to go running, with gentle footpaths snaking through the open fields and along the waterfront. There's a cool outdoor gym area whose rough-hewn weight machines are built of wood, like a Tinker Toy set designed for giants. Cycling paths go everywhere. There's a volleyball court and a skate park, although I might stick to my role as spectator on that one. Speaking of which, this is also a nice place to plop down on a blanket or a park bench and watch kayakers paddle by. And if you're travelling with kids, this park has a great playground. In the middle of the park there's a terrace bar-cafe with boule/ bocce courts, light meals and drinks.

# 3 NATURKOMPANIET

Hantverkargatan 38–40
08 651 35 00
www.naturkompaniet.se
Open Mon–Fri 10am–6pm,
Sat 10am–3pm
[MAP p. 156 C3]

Stockholmers, and Swedes in general, are very active, outdoorsy types, and if you have the opportunity to join them, you'll want to be ready. This shop carries everything you'll need for an epic outdoor adventure – warm clothes, sturdy boots, camping gear and, especially, those ubiquitous, highly coveted, quintessentially Swedish little Fjällraven backpacks in every possible colour. The shop also has good advice on places in and near the city to go hiking and camping, rock climbing, paddling, fishing, trail running, mountain biking, bird watching, mushroom hunting, and more, plus all the relevant maps and guidebooks. It's also a great place to find clothing and shoes designed for city backpacking.

**POCKET TIP**
For good hiking, head to Tyresta National Park, a 5000-acre primeval forest with 55 kilometres of trails, 20 kilometres from Stockholm.

# 4 VÄSTERMALMS GALLERIAN

Sankt Eriksgatan 45–51
08 696 30 31
www.vastermalmsgallerian.se
Open Mon–Fri 10am–7pm, Sat
10am–5pm, Sun 11am–5pm
[MAP p. 156 B1]

Normally I'm allergic to shopping centres but they're actually cool in Stockholm, possibly because the cold, damp weather makes it unpleasant to be outdoors for half the year. This one, like most in the city, is both a local hub of activity and a stylish collection of stores with well-designed and flatteringly lit public spaces. If the weather is bleak, duck into a cafe for your fika (afternoon coffee break). I like **Espresso House** and **Gateau**, plus there's a juice bar, a couple of sandwich joints, and a sushi bar. (Swedes have no issues with chain stores or chain restaurants, and it's hard to argue with consistent quality.) For kids' clothing, check out the Swedish-designed outfits at **Polarn O. Pyret**, whose clothes are known for being as rugged as they are cute. For cleverly designed gadgets, toys, novelties and travel accessories, pop into **Flying Tiger**, a Danish chain. Still raining? You can also get your hair and nails done, and pick up some groceries.

# 5 PHIL'S BURGER

Fleminggatan 49
08 408 840 80
www.philsburger.se
Open Mon–Thurs 11am–10pm,
Fri–Sat 11am–11pm, Sun
11am–9pm
[MAP p. 156 C2]

Stockholm became obsessed with American-style cheeseburgers a few years ago, and this is one of the small chains that popped up to perfect the Swedish interpretation of the form. Phil's keeps it simple: hand-shaped patties of farm-raised Swedish beef, house-baked organic bread, cheese and caramelised onions if you like, and some kind of magic sauce that makes these basic ingredients taste really, really good. The decor is equally simple: no frills, just basic, modern Scandinavian furnishings and fixtures. Vegan burgers, haloumi burgers and gluten-free buns are available, and, if you're brave, you can try the Beyond Burger, a plant-based patty that mimics the look and texture of ground beef. Get the sweet potato fries with extra Phil's sauce.

## 6 MÄLARPAVILJONGEN

Norr Mälarstrand 64
08 650 87 01
www.malarpaviljongen.se
Open 11am–1am (Apr–Sept)
[MAP p. 156 B3]

If you don't happen to have
a friend who owns a boat in
Stockholm and invites you
out for a drinks and dinner
cruise, this LGBTIQ-friendly
floating bar and restaurant is
a wonderful substitute. Open
in summer only, it's composed
of a series of awnings and
pagodas on floating docks,
adjoining a herb and flower
garden with additional
seating. Everything is leafy
and green and covered in
flowers. On a sunny afternoon
or evening, it's glorious. The
food is nothing astounding
but reliably good (I like the
burger and the grilled salmon
salad), but the cocktails are
outstanding; try a strawberry
margarita or a champagne
cocktail. Many of the staff are
expats or immigrants, and
all of them are intimidatingly
good-looking and disarmingly
friendly. There's live music on
most nights. If the atmosphere
inspires you, there's a garden
shop next-door.

**POCKET TIP**

Mälarpaviljongen
donates to and works
with the Regnbågsfonden
(Rainbow Fund), a charity
devoted to lesbian, gay,
bisexual and transgender
rights worldwide.

## 7 BILJARDPALATSET

Sankt Eriksgatan 52
08 652 51 00
biljardpalatset.se
Open Sun–Thurs 11am–1am,
Fri–Sat 11am–3am
[MAP p. 156 B1]

Although the name of this place is 'Billiard Palace,' and it does in fact have a vast room full of billiard and pool tables – not to mention a whole other room packed with full-size shuffleboard tables – that's not the coolest thing about it. The real draw (for me, at least) is the upstairs pinball hall (or flipper in Swedish). It's the largest line-up of flipper machines in the city, with a rotating cast of 20 games, both vintage and brand-new, plus five video games. Grab a beer and a handful of tokens downstairs, and see which one you can make last the longest. I know first-hand that the bartender might mock you, but only gently, if you burn through the tokens before you finish your beer, so get plenty.

# STOCKHOLM ARCHIPELAGO

Half the population of Stockholm fantasises about spending the summer in a little red cabin on a windswept, rocky island in the archipelago (for around 50,000 lucky souls who own cabins here, the dream is real). Depending on who's counting, the archipelago includes anywhere between 14,000 and 30,000 islands and skerries (small rocky islands), extending out about 60 kilometres (37 miles) east of the city into the Baltic Sea. The wilder, more remote islands like Finnhamn and Utö offer excellent cycling, swimming and nature walks, while closer-in Vaxholm is a seafood-lover's dream. You can see many of the islands on daytrips from Stockholm but to really soak up the restorative atmosphere, you should spend at least one night, and ideally several on one or more of the islands. Hire a little red cabin, or book a room in one of the many archipelago hostels.

Ferries go to most of the islands in summer and less frequently in winter (when ice blocks some of the routes). Waxholmsbolaget (www.waxholmsbolaget.se) is the main ferry operator, with the Strömkajen ferry terminal in front of the Grand Hotel (Södra Blasieholmshamnen 8) in Stockholm. An online trip-planner or smartphone app can help you plan a route; I tend to make a plan based on where the hostels are. A ferry pass is good for five days and costs SEK420. Single trips are SEK50 to SEK150, depending on distance. Always reserve accommodation, especially in summer, and take some groceries as business hours can be short and some islands don't have many services.

→ *The harbour at Finnhamn in the Stockholm Archipelago*

## VAXHOLM

The gateway to the archipelago, Vaxholm is easily accessible from Stockholm and makes a charming half-day excursion. You can even drive or take the bus here, although the ferry is more romantic. Stop in for a seafood lunch at the prominent **Waxholms Hotell**, then stroll the pretty streets lined with rickety, brightly painted wooden houses. Vaxholm made its name by supplying famously delicious herring to restaurants all over Sweden, but it started as a military outpost. Tours of the 16th-century **Vaxholm Fortress**, built by King Gustav Vasa, detail the history of the archipelago's important role in defending Stockholm. Boats go frequently from the Vaxholm harbour to the fortress year-round.

Waxholmsbolaget ferries (*see* p. 112) leave from Stockholm's Strömkajen ferry terminal (in front of the Grand Hotel) frequently for the one-hour trip. Bus 670 from the Tekniska Högskolan tunnelbana (train) station takes 45 minutes (and is covered by your local SL Access transit card). It's easy to continue from here to another island, as many of the ferry lines call at Vaxholm on their way out to further-flung places.

## FINNHAMN

This untamed, hiker-friendly island consists mostly of nature reserves, with good odds of spotting wildlife like foxes, badgers and tiny Swedish roe deer along its network of trails. There are great swimming and sunbathing nooks all around the island, whether you like your beaches sandy or made of smooth rock. It has an excellent hostel, called **Utsikt**, in a creaky old wooden building with good facilities – a massive dining hall where you can buy a hearty buffet breakfast, a large guest kitchen, nice showers, a TV lounge and a barbecue grill – and a fantastic view (the hostel's name means 'view'). In summer, the incongruously chic **Finnhamns Restaurant** near the ferry dock serves delicious seafood, and on summer weekends it opens up the rooftop bar with live music. A year-round shop next door to the restaurant sells basic groceries, ice-cream and coffee; you can also hire bicycles, kayaks, stand-up paddleboards (SUPs) and cabins here.

Ferries from Stockholm to Finnhamn take around two hours and depart from the piers at Slussen, Strömkajen or Strandvägen, depending on the season.

## UTÖ

Great for cycling, paddling, walking and sunning yourself on smooth, flat rocks, this former mining community is one of the largest and southernmost islands in the archipelago. In addition to the old mine, which has grown picturesque with neglect, it has a hostel attached to a more upscale hotel and restaurant (**Utö Värdshus**), small apartment-cabins you can stay in (all booked through the Värdshus), and a handful of cafes and bakeries in the village of Gruvbryggan, including the **Utö Bageri** (bakery) that has good organic coffee and, in my opinion, the best cardamom buns in all of Sweden. You can hire bicycles, kayaks or canoes at a kiosk in the village and spend the day circling the island, stopping at the various rocky inlets and outcroppings to sunbathe, picnic or just nap. Don't miss **Rävstavik**, an impressive set of rock formations at a beach 1.5 miles from the village along a well-signed path.

Boats from Stockholm take about three hours and dock at Gruvbryggan, the main village. There's a tourist information kiosk in a little red wooden hut, where you can pick up ideas about fun things to do.

# DROTTNINGHOLM PALACE

Drottningholm Palace was traditionally the summer residence of the royal family but since the 1980s the current king and queen have used it as their primary home – and who can blame them? The palace is gorgeous, set among lovely gardens on an island called Lovön, which sits in Lake Mälaren. The palace is about 10 kilometres outside of Stockholm and a popular daytrip. The boat ride from the city centre makes for a magical excursion.

The palace was designed by Nicodemus Tessin the Elder at the direction of Queen Hedwig Eleonora. Construction began in 1662, but Tessin died just before it was completed, so his son (imaginatively called Nicodemus Tessin the Younger) completed it. You can stroll the grounds on your own, but it's worth springing for a 45-minute tour (SEK30 per person), where guides tell stories that bring the place to life.

Boats run by Strömma Kanalbolaget (www.stromma.se/en/Stockholm) depart frequently from the Stadshuskajen quay outside Stockholm's City Hall. There's also a well-marked bicycle path that leads here from the city centre; find it outside Fridhemsplan tunnelbana (train) station. Or take the tunnelbana to Brommaplan, then transfer to the bus marked 'Drottningholm'.

→ Drottningholm Palace

## GARDENS & THEATRE

The gardens surrounding the palace come from several different time periods including 17th-century Baroque and consequently embody various styles. Some sections are formal, with manicured shrubs, tidy avenues of trees and elaborate sculptures, fountains and pools. The garden's outlying areas are left more natural, so that the garden as a whole feels integrated with the surrounding landscape. And then there are labyrinths (especially fun – or scary – for kids short enough to feel lost inside them). Happily, there are also park benches scattered around to rest weary feet, as it's a lot of ground to cover.

Another highlight of a visit to Drottningholm is touring the theatre. Built in 1766, it is still used for opera performances today, including all of the original theatre machinery. The interior makes use of the architectural equivalent of stage make-up, using things like papier-mâché to create the look of much more expensive building materials. But the best part is backstage where elaborate machinery is used to quickly change scenes, create the effect of a rolling ocean floor and imitate a thunder and lightning storm with a mechanical thunder machine and candle sconces.

## CHINE/E PAVILION (KINA /LOTT)

This whimsical leisure palace on the Drottningholm grounds is another highlight of visiting. It was a surprise birthday gift in 1753 to the Swedish queen Lovisa Ulrika from her king, Adolf Frederick; their son, then seven-year-old crown prince, who would grow up to become King Gustav III, handed her the golden key. The original structure wasn't built to last, but the queen loved it, so when it started to fall apart she had it replaced with a sturdier version. The Rococo building is done up in Sweden's interpretation of Chinese decor – lacquered wall panels, vases and screens – which was extremely fashionable at the time. The Swedish East India Company had given Swedes a glimpse of luxurious products like silk and porcelain, and everyone who was anyone wanted to have a Chinese-style room to show off.

Just north of the Chinese pavilion is a separate building housing a dining room with a special feature: the kitchen and dining room table are below ground-level, so the laden table could have been hoisted up to the ground floor where the hungry nobles awaited their meal. When they were finished, back down it went, dirty dishes and all – no chance of gossipy servants listening in on conversations.

123

**FIELD TRIP**

# UPPSALA

The lively city of Uppsala, just north of Stockholm, is a fun college town with a thriving cafe culture, bicycles and parks everywhere, and a lazy river slinking through its centre. But it's also an ideal place to steep yourself in Swedish history. Uppsala University is the oldest in the country, founded in 1477. The castle, a hulking pink fortress on top of a hill above town, was built in 1549 by Sweden's favourite king, Gustav Vasa, and it's where Queen Christina abdicated the throne in 1654. At least one ancient thinker, Olof Rudbeck, believed Uppsala was really the lost city of Atlantis.

Buses and trains go frequently from Stockholm to Uppsala. Or you can catch a regional commuter train from Stockholm Central Station to Uppsala Central Station (40 minutes). Buy train tickets at ticket machines or the SL ticket office at the station. Flixbus (www.flixbus.se) runs direct buses hourly from Stockholm's central bus station, reaching Uppsala Central Station (1 hour, 15 minutes). For the best price, buy tickets online; tickets from bus drivers are full-price (cash only).

3

→ *The river Fyris makes its way through the middle of Uppsala*

## GAMLA UPP/ALA /IGHT/

About six kilometers north of Uppsala's city centre is **Gamla (Old) Uppsala**, one of the most important ancient burial sites in Sweden. The main attraction here are three large **burial mounds** from the 5th and 6th centuries, which excavations show contain human remains as well as ivory, jewels and other evidence of early trading routes. The burial mounds look just like green hills; in fact, during the 1950s people used to ski on them in winter. Such disrespect! These days, fences discourage visitors from walking on the mounds unless they're part of a tour, but you can get pretty close. For an inside view, head to the **Gamla Uppsala Museum**, which explains the significance of the burial mounds, describing the people they might contain and what the world was like when their occupants lived here. Included in the Gamla Uppsala area is **Disagården**, an open-air museum full of pretty wooden farm buildings. You can also peek into the **Gamla Uppsala kyrka** (old church), built in the 12th century – some say atop the ruins of a pagan temple.

Legend has it that Swedish king Erik Jedvardsson, patron saint of Stockholm, walked out of the Gamla Uppsala church one Sunday in the year 1160 and right into a battle with

the Danes, in which he was beheaded. The king's head rolled down a hill, and where it stopped, a spring bubbled up. Voila, sainthood. Each year, for centuries, Erik's remains were carried from their resting place in the 'new' Uppsala Cathedral (*see* p. 129) in the modern city to the old church at Gamla Uppsala, along a footpath called **Eriksleden** – still the best way to get from the heart of Uppsala to its historic birthplace. The **tourist office** in Uppsala has maps of the well-signposted footpath. You can also reach Gamla Uppsala by taking bus 2 from Uppsala's main square, Stora Torget (ticket machines are at the bus stop).

## UPPSALA SIGHTS

Back in modern Uppsala, stop in at the 'new' (circa 1270) **Uppsala Cathedral** as you stroll along the lovely Fyris River that bisects the city centre. Several kings are buried in the cathedral, along with botanist Carl Linnaeus and scientist Emanuel Swedenborg. Then walk uphill towards the **castle**, a corner of which is home to the **Uppsala Art Museum**. Along the way, stop in at **Carolina Rediviva**, the university library, for a peek at the Silver Bible and other precious maps and manuscripts displayed in a hallway near the entrance. And don't miss the **Gustavianum**, the university museum of antiquities and scientific history; it's charmingly creaky, and the dome on top holds a dizzying 17th-century anatomical theatre. Uppsala is also the home of botanist Carl Linnaeus (1707–1778), founder of the taxonomic system of naming plants and animals; you can visit his home, now the **Linnaeus Museum** (Svartbäcksgatan 27), surrounded by his own garden.

## UPPSALA SHOPPING & EATING

For bibliophiles, there's a vast selection of reading material – from literary fiction to history and politics – at the cosy **English Bookshop** (Svartbäcksgatan 19), which also hosts author readings and events. It's a friendly place and a social hub; the London Book Fair named it Bookshop of the Year in 2018. For gifts such as cleverly designed household gadgets, patterned linens, and handmade wooden and leather goods, check out **Designtorget** (Smedsgränd 8), on the lower level of **Åhléns** department store – itself a fine place to scout for uniquely Nordic design, like Marimekko coffee mugs, printed hand-towels, and fika (coffee) serving trays.

Stop for lunch or pick up some next-level take-away from **Hambergs Fisk** (Fyristorg 8), right along the river. You can choose from cured salmon (gravad lax), shrimp salad, Arctic char (röding) and more. Dinner here is more elaborate (you'll need reservations), with set menus and an epic wine list. There are also several restaurants inside the food hall **Saluhallen** (St Eriks Torg), between the river and the cathedral, including a sushi bar and a steakhouse.

## GETTING TO /TOCKHOLM

### Flying

Stockholm's main airport, Arlanda (ARN), is 37km (23 miles) north of the city centre. It has four terminals; 2 and 5 are used for international flights, 3 and 4 for domestic. Walkways connect the terminals. Between terminals 4 and 5 is Sky City, a walkway lined with shops and restaurants.

### Getting to/from the airport:
### Train

The Arlanda Express train (www. arlandaexpress.com) is the quickest and easiest way from the airport to the city centre. It takes 20 minutes and departs about every 15 minutes from well-marked stations in Arlanda North (Terminal 5) and Arlanda South (Terminals 2, 3 and 4) directly to Stockholm Central Station. Tickets are SEK280 (round-trip SEK540), bought from machines in the terminal before you board.

Commuter trains (pendeltåg) that run between Stockholm Central and Uppsala Central also stop on the way at Arlanda Central (the stop at Arlanda is outside of Sky City). The journey to the city centre takes about 40 minutes. Tickets cost SEK151, which includes an airport supplement. For a cheaper option, you can also take Bus 583 from Arlanda (any terminal) to the Märsta train station, then buy a single ticket for the commuter train from Märsta to Stockholm Central (SEK33–41).

### Bus

Airport buses (Flygbussarna) go from the airport to Stockholm's central bus station, departing every 10 minutes from each of the airport terminals. The journey takes about 45 minutes. Tickets cost SEK119 one-way, SEK215 round-trip, bought from machines in the terminals.

### Taxi

Taxi companies all have a similar fixed-price fare to and from the airport (usually SEK450–500).

## GETTING AROUND /TOCKHOLM

### Tickets

The train and buses are run by SL (http://sl.se) – the same passes and tickets work for both and also on local Stockholm ferries.

There are several options for tickets; which one you choose will depend on how long you're staying and how much walking you like to do. If you plan to use public transport a lot, it's worth getting a refillable SL Access card (SEK20), which you can buy at the SL Center inside Central Station and in tunnelbana (train) stations: T-Centralen, Gullmarsplan, Fridhemsplan and Tekniska högskolan, or in Pressbyrån or 7-Eleven shops, then load it with as many credits as you like (either when you purchase or at automated machines in bus and tunnelbana stations). Tap it each time you board a bus or enter a tunnelbana station. SL also has a smartphone app through which you can buy tickets. For most travellers, the best bet is to buy a travel card, good for unlimited travel for 24 hours (SEK125), 72 hours (SEK250) or 7 days (SEK325), on all SL buses and trains. (The 7-day pass requires buying an SL Access card first and loading it up.)

Single tickets (good for 75 minutes) are available at ticket machines (SEK44), but not always near bus stations, and you can't buy tickets on board the bus, so plan ahead. Prices are discounted for people over age 65 and under age 20. Bicycles are not allowed on the train.

Penalties for not carrying a valid ticket are steep (around SEK1500), and SL officials do check frequently, so don't risk trying to cheat the system.

### Bus

Stockholm's buses are clean, prompt and ubiquitous; they go pretty much everywhere you're likely to want to go and are a pleasant way to see the city while getting around.

### Tram

The No. 7 tram that goes between Norrmalm and Djurgården operates on the SL network, just like the bus and tunnelbana systems. SL Access cards or single SL tickets work; buy them before you board. (There are ticket machines at the tram stops.)

### Tunnelbana

The tunnelbana (train) system typically runs like clockwork. Stations are marked with a large blue T, and most have multiple entrances, which can be confusing when you exit. To avoid ending up several blocks from your destination, there's almost always a map on the wall on train platforms, with each exit (and nearby major streets) highlighted, so you can know at-a-glance which direction to walk in if you happen not to have checked ahead. As you stop at many of the city's train stations you'll see they have been painted or decorated with murals and installations by well-known Scandinavian artists; a brochure available at the tourist information centre leads you on a self-guided tour of them.

### Ferries

SL Access and travel cards also cover travel on Stockholm ferries, which go from Gamla Stan (at Skeppsbron) and from Norrmalm (at Nybroplan) to the park island of Djurgården, about every 15 minutes in summer, less frequently the rest of the year. Ferries to and through the Stockholm archipelago operate on a separate network, with passes and single-trip tickets available on board or in advance through Waxholmsbolaget (*see* p.112; www.waxholmsbolaget.se).

### Bicycle

Cycling around Stockholm is extremely popular, and a great way to see large areas in a short time. The city is mostly flat, with bike lanes as well as dedicated bike paths. Traffic in central Stockholm can be chaotic, but cyclists and pedestrians have de facto priority. Helmets are required for children age 15 and under. Bikeshare programs include CityBikes (www.citybikes.se), which offers three-day cards for SEK165; purchase from 7-Eleven, Pressbyrån shops or tourist offices, then pick up a bike from a CityBikes station and return it to any other CityBike station.

### Walking

Stockholm has a compact core and is so picturesque that walking is a great way to get around. Depending on where you're going, it can be quicker than taking the tunnelbana (train), especially if you factor in all the walking through underground stations.

### Taxi

Three main taxi companies operate in Stockholm:

Taxi 020 (www.sverigetaxi.se/)

Taxi Kurir (www.taxikurir.se)

Taxi Stockholm (www.taxistockholm.se)

There are other independent companies, but unlike the three listed companies, their prices may vary wildly, so be sure to agree on a fare before hopping in. Taxis can be hailed from the street or booked by phone or online. Uber and other rideshare services also operate in Stockholm.

## CLIMATE

Stockholm has a mild, humid climate; its generally warm but short summers (June–August) consist of long days, with up to 18 hours of daylight, while winter days can have as few as six hours of daylight. Most people visit in summer, as the weather is beautiful and attractions are open longer hours. In winter, prepare to bundle up, stop often for hot beverages and develop a love of candlelight.

## TIME ZONES

Sweden is on Central European Time (GMT+2).

## PHONES

The country code for Sweden is +46. The area code for Stockholm is 08 (drop the 0 if calling internationally). In emergencies, dial 112. The non-emergency police line is 114 14.

If you have an unlocked mobile phone, you can buy a prepaid SIM card at Pressbyrån convenience stores (including at the airport) or mobile-phone provider shops when you get to Stockholm and use your phone as normal, with a local number. SIM cards can be reloaded with credit at Pressbyrån stores as well as any mobile-phone provider shops (companies include Telia, Comviq and 3). Although not specific to Stockholm, another option is to leave your phone on airplane mode, with wi-fi on, which lets you use things like maps and email (but not cellular data).

## WI-FI & ELECTRICITY

Wi-fi is free to use at nearly every coffee shop, library, and museum. In places where a password is required, it's usually printed on your receipt.
Voltage 230V, Europlug type C and F (two round prongs).

## MEDIA & TOURIST INFORMATION

Stockholm's main visitor information center is inside Kulturhuset (Sergels Torg 3–5), the large, modern cultural centre near Sergels Torg in Norrmalm. It's open Mon–Fri 9am–6pm (to 7pm in summer), Sat 9am–4pm (to 6pm in summer) and Sun 10am–4pm. See www.touristinfo@stockholm.se

## PUBLIC HOLIDAYS & FESTIVALS

### Midsummer

The second biggest holiday in Sweden (after Christmas), Midsummer Day, held on a Saturday in June, is a clear holdover from Sweden's pagan past. Women put wildflowers in their hair, and everyone sings and dances around a maypole. The main festivities are held on Midsummer's Eve (Friday), with Saturday devoted to recovering from the party. Midsummer marks the start of the summer season; many visitor-centric attractions (including ferries, restaurants and hostels in the Stockholm archipelago) operate on limited schedules until Midsummer. From midday on Midsummer Eve through the weekend, the entire city shuts down – even museums are closed and most Stockholmers leave town to celebrate. For those who stay in Stockholm, the biggest party happens at Skansen, the open-air museum on Djurgården.

### Summer holidays

Top restaurants typically close for a few weeks in summer, usually mid-July to mid-August.

### Winter holidays

On St Lucia Day (13 December), the festival of lights, young girls wear crowns of burning candles and lead processions to a church, singing traditional songs. It's meant to help lift the December gloom and kick off the Christmas season. Closely associated with the holiday are lussekatte (saffron buns).

The big Christmas celebration is held 24 December, Christmas Eve. The Julbord, or traditional Christmas smörgåsbord, is an elaborate affair involving many rounds of eating and drinking. At 3pm on Christmas Eve, all over Sweden, families sit down reverently in front of the TV to watch *Kalle Anka* (Donald Duck), an annual program of short, vintage Disney cartoons that has been shown since the 1960s.

## EATING & DRINKING

Traditional Swedish cooking is known as husmanskost: think meatballs or fried Baltic herring with potatoes and lingonberries. Other examples include Wallenbergare, a meat patty dish made from ground veal, cream and eggs, breaded and served with mashed potatoes, peas and lingonberries; pytt i panna, a Swedish potato hash served with a fried egg and beets; and pea soup with pancakes, traditionally served on Thursdays. Also, look for open-face shrimp sandwiches (räksmörgås), cured salmon (gravlax) and pickled herring (inlagd sill). August brings crayfish parties, as well as surströmming, a pungent specialty of fermented pickled herring that is very much an acquired taste. Try it at your own risk and have plenty of aquavit ready to wash it down!

Modern cuisine in Stockholm tends to play with these same dishes, adding twists and flavours from international cultures. Seasonal, local and sustainable ingredients are all apparent in Stockholm's many cafes and restaurants. Various ethnic cuisines are also easy to find, especially Thai, Italian, Indian, Middle Eastern and Japanese.

Most restaurants, including exclusive and upscale places, offer a cheaper menu from 11am to 2pm, called dagens lunch (daily lunch), usually including a main meal plus salad, bread and coffee. Most people have lunch between 11.30am and 1.30pm, and dinner from 6pm to around 9pm.

It's not cheating to have lunch in the cafeteria at a museum. We used to joke that anytime we visited a museum, my grandmother made a beeline for the cafe, but in fact most museums have excellent restaurants worth a visit in their own right.

### Drinks

Alcohol is expensive in Sweden, though not as outrageously so as in the pre-EU days. It's sold and regulated by the state monopoly, Systembolaget, whose shops are marked by green and yellow signs. Craft brewing has taken off in Sweden, which is a good thing, as mass-produced Swedish beer has little to recommend it. Hard cider is increasingly popular. As for hard booze, Sweden's specialty is aquavit, a distilled liquor similar to vodka spiced with caraway and other flavours, served in shots (nubbe) and often accompanied by drinking songs. There's also Swedish punsch, a strongly flavoured liqueur made with arrack.

## MONEY & ATMS

Although Sweden is part of the EU, it voted in 2003 to stick with the krona, not adopt the euro. Kronor are made up of öre, although prices are essentially always rounded up to the nearest krona.

ATMs are common in town and at the airport, bus and train stations. Most require a 4-digit PIN code. Be hesitant to withdraw too much cash, though, as you might have trouble spending it: more and more places are switching to cash-free payment systems. Often, this means you'll need to use an app or send an SMS to pay for basic things like parking or public restrooms. For restrooms, this is exactly as frustrating as it sounds, and my only advice is to plan well ahead so that you have time to find an alternative (e.g. ask for change or find a friendly cafe). For parking, it's worth downloading the free smartphone app Betala P, available for Android and iOS, which lets you pay with your phone via a linked credit card or Paypal.

To use a debit or credit card, you'll usually need a PIN code. If your card doesn't have one, the salesperson might ask you to sign a receipt and show your driver's license or ID.

## GREEN STOCKHOLM

Environmentally friendly practices are the norm in Stockholm. Locally grown, sustainable produce, fish and game are valued and used whenever possible; hotels and hostels provide sorting bins for garbage; and Stockholm's famously clean water is such a visible and important element of the city's beauty that ecologically sound behaviour makes perfect sense.

## SHOPPING

While many shops in Stockholm still accept cash, cash-free transactions are becoming much more popular, a trend that's likely to continue. Using a credit card without a PIN code means you'll generally need to show ID and sign a receipt.

Bargaining isn't really done here, even in places like flea markets and produce markets.

Non-EU residents are eligible for tax-free shopping in Sweden, for purchases of at least SEK200. The standard VAT rate is 25 per cent, so it's worth doing the paperwork. Ask for a Global Blue Tax Free Shopping form when you make your purchase; fill it out and have it stamped when you go through customs at the airport as you leave Sweden. (You'll need to show your original receipt, passport and the items you bought – unused.) You can get an immediate refund from a Global Blue agent (in terminals 2 and 5 at Arlanda Airport) or mail the stamped forms to Global Blue's office within 90 days.

Most credit card companies will charge a foreign-transaction fee; if you're expecting to do a lot of shopping, it might be worth applying for a travel-friendly card that waives these.

## ACCOMMODATION

Hotels are of a high standard, though rooms tend to be smaller (which is typically European) than what you'd find in equivalent hotels, particularly in the US. Most hotels include an expansive breakfast buffet in the price.

Hostels in Sweden operate more like budget hotels. They're called vandrarhem (wanderers' homes), and aren't particularly youth-focused. Most offer private rooms, sometimes with en suite bathrooms. There's usually an optional extra charge for bedding, towels and breakfast.

**Recommended hotels:**

**Hobo Hotel** (www.hobo.se) Budget-friendly rooms, plus a cool bar and rooftop restaurant called Tak.

**Långholmen Hotel & Hostel** (www.langholmen.com) Rooms in a renovated former prison building.

**Hotel C** (www.hotelcstockholm.com) Home of the Ice Bar; inches from the Arlanda Express train to the airport; great facilities, good budget-room options.

**Hotel Rival** (www.rival.se/en) Boutique hotel with pop prestige, co-owned by ABBA's Benny Andersson.

Booking an apartment through Airbnb is generally less expensive than a hotel, and it gives you a base in a residential neighbourhood and the opportunity to cook some of your own meals.

## TIPPING

In general, gratuities are figured into the bill in Swedish restaurants, bars and hotels. For excellent service, a tip of 10–15 percent is appreciated. In taxis, you can round up the bill, but tipping is not required.

## ETIQUETTE

Stockholmers queue up for everything. It's not unheard of to see people standing in line in order to take a number from the queue machine so they can stand in line. Jump the queue at your peril.

## LANGUAGE

Most Swedes speak fluent English and enjoy a chance to practice with native speakers, but learning a few Swedish words will usually win you a smile. When in doubt, throw in a tack (thanks) – it's the all-purpose glue that holds society together.

### Phrase Guide

**Hej/Hej då** Hello/goodbye

**Tack** Thanks

**Var så god** You're welcome

**Ursäkta mig** Excuse me

**Forlåt** Sorry/Pardon me

**Stängt** Closed

**Lagom** A Swedish word that doesn't have an exact equivalent in English but roughly speaking, it means 'not too little, not too much, but just enough.'

## INDIGENOUS SAMI PEOPLE

The Sami people are indigenous to Sápmi (often called Lapland), a territory that stretches across parts of northern Sweden, Norway, Finland and into Russia's Kola Peninsula. Sami culture has historically revolved around reindeer herding, and traditional Sami handicrafts such as reindeer-horn knives and cups, wire-embroidered leather goods and woven birch baskets are highly valued as gifts.

## EMBASSIES

**Australia**
Klarabergsviadukten 63
08-613 29 00
www.sweden.embassy.gov.au

**UK**
Skarpögatan 6
08-671 30 00
www.gov.uk/government/world/organisations/british-embassy-stockholm

**United States**
Dag Hammarskjölds väg 31
08-783 53 00
www.se.usembassy.gov

**Canada**
Klarabergsgatan 23
08-453 30 00
www.canadainternational.gc.ca/sweden-suede/

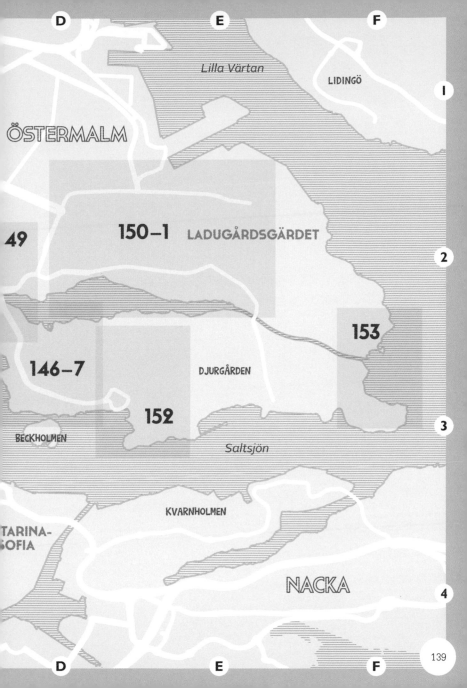

*Lilla Värtan*

LIDINGÖ

ÖSTERMALM

**49**

**150–1** LADUGÅRDSGÄRDET

**153**

**146–7**

DJURGÅRDEN

**152**

BECKHOLMEN

*Saltsjön*

KVARNHOLMEN

TARINA-
SOFIA

NACKA

**D**  **E**  **F**

LEJONBACKEN

SKEPPSBRON

Inre
Borggården

**LIVRUSTKAMMAREN**
(ROYAL ARMOURY)

**I**

Yttre
Borggården

SKEPPSBRON

Högvaktsterrassen

KUNGLIGA
SLOTTET
(ROYAL PALACE)

Karl XIV Johan
statue

Slottsbacken

TELEGRAFGRÄND

BOLLHUSGRÄND

SKEPPAR KARLS GRÄND

**2**

Olaus Petri
statue

**Storkyrkan**
(Great Church)

**Finska Kyrkan**
(Finnish Church)

KRÅKGRÄND

Storkyrkans
Gård

Järnpojke
(Iron Boy statue)

Sankt Göran
och Draken
(St George &
the Dragon statue)

NYGRÄND

**Börshuset**

TRÄDGÅRDSGATAN

Castle
House
Inn

**NOBELMUSEET**
(NOBEL MUSEUM)

KÖPMANGATAN

BRUNNSGRÄND

Hotell
Gyllene
Geten

**STORTORGET**
(MAIN SQUARE)

**GRILLSKA
HUSETS
KONDITORI**

SKOTTGRÄND

**UNDER
KASTANJEN**

**HILDA
HILDA**

**3**

PRÄSTGATAN

SKOMAKARGATAN

SVARTMANGATAN

**STUDIO
LENA M**

STORA HOPAREGRÄND

KINDSTUGATAN

SJÄLAGÅRDSGATAN

BAGGENSGATAN

DRAKENS   GRÄND

ÖSTERLÅNGGATAN

FERKENS GRÄND

Hotell
Skeppsbron

**KERSTIN
ADOLPHSON
BUTIK**

SVARTMANGATAN

**Tyska
Kyrkan**
(German Church)

PELIKANSGRÄND

TYSKA BRINKEN

PRÄSTGATAN

VÄSTERLÅNGGATAN

**SÖDERMALM**

JOHANNESGRÄND

**4**

Junotäppan

**D**  **E**  **F**

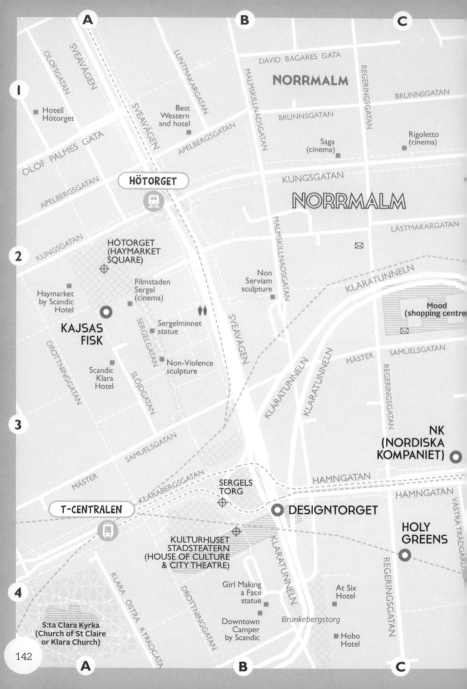

A1 — SVEAVÄGEN, OLOFSGATAN, LUNTMAKARGATAN, OLOF PALMES GATA, APELBERGSGATAN, Hotell Hötorget

B1 — DAVID BAGARES GATA, NORRMALM, MALMSKILLNADSGATAN, BRUNNSGATAN, Best Western and hotel, APELBERGSGATAN

C1 — REGERINGSGATAN, BRUNNSGATAN, Saga (cinema), Rigoletto (cinema)

HÖTORGET

KUNGSGATAN

NORRMALM

A2 — KUNGSGATAN, HÖTORGET (HAYMARKET SQUARE), Haymarket by Scandic Hotel, KAJSAS FISK, Filmstaden Sergel (cinema), Sergelminnet statue, DROTTNINGGATAN, SERGELGATAN, SLÖJDGATAN, Scandic Klara Hotel, Non-Violence sculpture

B2 — Non Serviam sculpture, MALMSKILLNADSGATAN, SVEAVÄGEN

C2 — LÄSTMAKARGATAN, KLARATUNNELN, Mood (shopping centre)

A3 — SAMUELSGATAN, MÄSTER

B3 — KLARATUNNELN

C3 — MÄSTER SAMUELSGATAN, REGERINGSGATAN, NK (NORDISKA KOMPANIET)

T-CENTRALEN

SERGELS TORG

HAMNGATAN

DESIGNTORGET

HOLY GREENS

A4 — KLARA ÖSTRA KYRKOGATA, S:ta Clara Kyrka (Church of St Claire or Klara Church)

B4 — KULTURHUSET STADSTEATERN (HOUSE OF CULTURE & CITY THEATRE), KLARABERGSGATAN, DROTTNINGGATAN, Girl Making a Face statue, Downtown Camper by Scandic, KLARATUNNELN

C4 — At Six Hotel, Brunkebergstorg, Hobo Hotel, REGERINGSGATAN, HAMNGATAN, VÄSTRA TRÄDGÅRDSGATAN

D

*Humlegården*

E

F

BIRGER JARLSGATAN

Hotel Drottning Kristina

Scandic Anglais Hotel

nnsgatan

atre)

SPY BAR

HUMLEGÅRDSGATAN

GREVTUREGATAN

MAJORSGATAN

NYBROGATAN

**1**

Hotel Kung Carl

KUNGSGATAN

SVAMPEN

**HEDENGRENS**

**STUREHOF**

0 ——— 100 m

**ÖSTERMALM**

**ÖSTERMALMS SALUHALL**

**SVENSK HEMSLÖJD**

JAKOBSBERGSGATAN

GREVTUREGATAN

N

Eldhs Fontän

**STUREKATTEN**

RIDDARGATAN

**2**

NYBROGATAN

SIBYLLEGATAN

**ÖSTERMALMSTORG**

MÄSTER SAMUELSGATAN

BIBLIOTEKSGATAN

**WIENER CAFÉET**

NORRLANDSGATAN

INGMAR BERGMANS GATA

SMÅLANDSGATAN

Hotel Riddargatan

Hotell Örnsköld

Dramatens Lilla scenen (theatre)

RIDDARGATAN

Scenkonstmuseet (Swedish Museum of Performing Arts)

BIRGER JARLSGATAN

NYBROGATAN

*Norrmalmstorg*

Nobis Hotel

Frihetens Källa sculpture

Laura sculpture

**NORRMALMSTORG**

Hallwylska Museet

Margaretha Krook statue

**DRAMATEN (ROYAL DRAMATIC THEATRE)**

H.M. Konungens Hovstall (Royal Stables)

**3**

KUNGSTRÄDGÅRDEN

KUNGSTRÄDGÅRDSGATAN

NÄCKSTRÖMSGATAN

China Teatern (theatre)

Berns Hotel

**NYBROPLAN**

VÄPNARGATAN

Berzelius statue

*Berzelii Park*

Raoul Wallenbergstorg

**SVENSKT TENN**

STRANDVÄGEN

**NYBROKAJEN**

**STRANDVÄGEN**

KUNGSTRÄDGÅRDEN

WAHRENDORFFSGATAN

*Nybroviken*

**KUNGSTRÄDGÅRDEN**

ARSENALSGATAN

NYBROKAJEN

Konstantinopelhästen statue

*Blasieholmstorg*

Radisson Collection Hotel

D

E

F

**4**

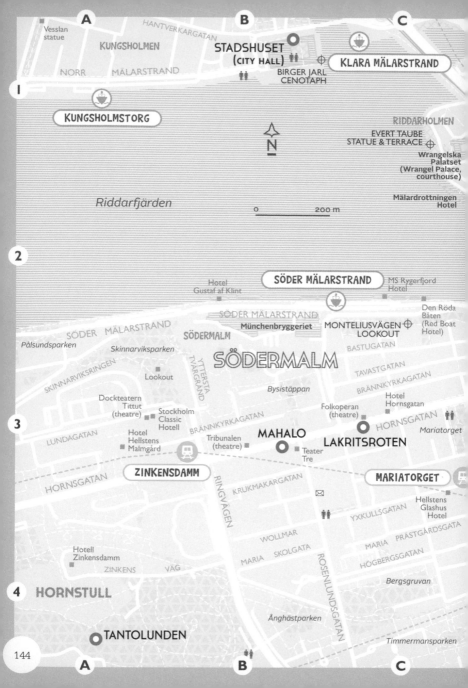

A · B · C

NORRMALM

Molins Fontän

**KUNGSTRÄDGÅRDEN**

Jakobs Kyrka (St James's Church)

Jakobs Torg

Karl XII statue

KUNGSTRÄDGÅRDEN

REGERINGSGATAN

MALMTORGSGATAN

JAKOBSGATAN

JAKOBS TORG

GUSTAV ADOLFS TORG

JAKOBS TORG

KARL XII:S TORG

KUNGSTRÄDGÅRDSGATAN

BIRGIT NILSSONS ALLÉ

**OPERAN**

Gustav Adolfs Torg

STRÖMGATAN

**MEDELHAVSMUSEET** (MEDITERRANEAN MUSEUM)

0 — 50 m

Norrström

STRÖMGATAN

STRÖMBRON

Strömparterren

Solsängaren statue

NORRBRO

Stockholms Medeltidsmuseum (Stockholm Medieval Museum)

N

Riksplan

**HELGEANDSHOLMEN**

SLOTTSKAJEN

LEJONBACKEN

SKEPPSBRON

**Riksdagshuset** (Parliament House)

RIKSGATAN

Museum Tre Kronor (Museum Three Crowns)

Gustav III:s antikmuseum (Gustav III Museum of Antiquities)

**SÖDERMALM**

Stallkanalen

SLOTTSKAJEN

LEJONBACKEN

BANKKAJEN

Inre Borggården

**LIVRUSTKAMMAREN** (ROYAL ARMOURY)

KANSLIKAJEN

Mynttorget

MYNTGATAN

**GAMLA STAN** STADSHOLMEN

Yttre Borggården

**KUNGLIGA SLOTTET** (ROYAL PALACE)

Högvaktsterrassen

Slottsbacken

Morgon statue

Brantingtorget

Karl XIV Johan statue

I · 1

2

3

4

145

A

B

C

1

Viewpoint

Junibacken
(Children's
Cultural
Centre)

Galärparken

NORDISKA
MUSEET
(NORDIC MUSEUM)

VASA
MUSEET
(VASA MUSEUM)

Galärvarvskyrkogården
(cemetery)

Ladugårdslandsviken

DJURGÅRD

Sjöhistoriska-
Museifartygen
(Maritime Museum)

SPRITMUSEUM

2

Teater
Galeasen

ÖSTRA BROBÄNKEN

SLUPSKJULSVÄGEN

MODERNA
MUSEET
(MODERN ART MUSEUM)

Wasahamnen
(Stockholm
Guest Harbour)

Vikingaliv
Museum

Sjöhistoriska
Båthall

ARKDES
(SWEDISH CENTRE
FOR ARCHITECTURE
AND DESIGN)

De Fyra
Elementen
(The Four
Elements
sculpture)

SVENSKSUNDSVÄGEN

3

Paradiset
sculptures

Svensksundsparken

LÅNGA    RADEN

Skeppsholmen
Hotel

SKEPPSHOLMEN

NORRMALM

SÖDRA    BROBÄNKEN

SKEPPSHOLMEN

ALLMÄNNA GRÄND

N

KASTELLBACKEN

KASTELLHOLMEN

ORLOGSVÄGEN

Viewpoint

4

0        100 m

A

B

C

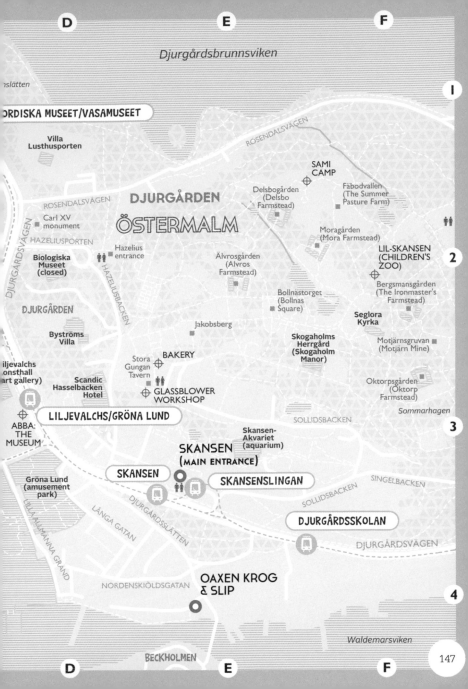

Djurgårdsbrunnsviken

...nslätten

**I**

**ORDISKA MUSEET/VASAMUSEET**

**Villa Lusthusporten**

ROSENDALSVÄGEN

**DJURGÅRDEN**

**ÖSTERMALM**

ROSENDALSVÄGEN

**Carl XV monument**

HAZELIUSPORTEN

**Hazelius entrance**

HAZELIUSBACKEN

**Biologiska Museu (closed)**

DJURGÅRDSVÄGEN

**DJURGÅRDEN**

**Byströms Villa**

**SAMI CAMP**

**Delsbogården (Delsbo Farmstead)**

**Fäbodvallen (The Summer Pasture Farm)**

**Moragården (Mora Farmstead)**

**Älvrosgården (Alvros Farmstead)**

**LIL-SKANSEN (CHILDREN'S ZOO)**

**2**

**Bergsmansgården (The Ironmaster's Farmstead)**

**Bollnästorget (Bollnas Square)**

**Seglora Kyrka**

**Jakobsberg**

**Skogaholms Herrgård (Skogaholm Manor)**

**Motjärnsgruvan (Motjärn Mine)**

**Stora Gungan Tavern**

**BAKERY**

**Scandic Hasselbacken Hotel**

**GLASSBLOWER WORKSHOP**

**Oktorpsgården (Oktorp Farmstead)**

*Sommarhagen*

**3**

**iljevalchs onsthall art gallery)**

**LILJEVALCHS/GRÖNA LUND**

SOLLIDSBACKEN

**ABBA: THE MUSEUM**

**Skansen-Akvariet (aquarium)**

**SKANSEN (MAIN ENTRANCE)**

**Gröna Lund (amusement park)**

**SKANSEN**

**SKANSENSLINGAN**

SOLLIDSBACKEN

SINGELBACKEN

LÄNGA GATAN

DJURGÅRDSSLÄTTEN

**DJURGÅRDSSKOLAN**

DJURGÅRDSVÄGEN

LILLA ALLMÄNNA GRAND

NORDENSKIÖLDSGATAN

**OAXEN KROG & SLIP**

**4**

*Waldemarsviken*

BECKHOLMEN

A
B
C

1

Systrarna statue
(The Sisters)

Sjöfartshotellet Hotel

KLEVGRÄND

KATARINAVÄGEN

STADSGÅRDSLEDEN

FOTOGRAFISKA

Mosebacke Torg

La Mano sculpture

HERMANS

SVARTENSGATAN

Teatre Dur & Moll

HÖGBERGSGATAN

KATARINA VASTRA KYRKOGATA

Katarina Kyrka
(Church of Catherine)

KATARINA ÖSTRA KYRKOGÅRDSGRÄND

NYTORGSGATAN

RENSTIERNAS GATA

ÖSTGÖTAGATAN

TJÄRHOVSGATAN

NOFO Hotel

Centrum för Fotografi (CFF)

2

TJÄRHOVSGATAN

Hotel Söder

Droskan

FOLKUNGAGATAN

KVARNEN

FOLKUNGAGATAN

Folkungakyrkan

KOCKSGATAN

RENSTIERNAS GATA

Scandic Malmen Hotel

SÖDERMALM

MEDBORGARPLATSEN

KATARINA SOFIA

Axel Landquists Park

Göta Lejon
(theatre)

ÅSÖGATAN

ÖSTGÖTAGATAN

NYTORGSGATAN

ÅSÖGATAN

KOCKSGATAN

BONDEGATAN

3

GÖTAGATAN

ÅSÖGATAN

SÖDERMALM

Victoria
(cinema)

BONDEGATAN

GRANDPA

BUS
(theatre)

URBAN DELI
NYTORGET

Nytorget

CHUTNEY

SKÅNEGATAN

SÖDERMANNAGATAN

Jannica med Dockvagnen statue
(Jannica with a doll's pram)

UGGLAN

KATARINA BANGATA

SOFIAGATAN

N

Nackas Hörna

0        100 m

Åsötorget

SÖDERMANNAGATAN

KATARINA BANGATA

4

GÖTAGATAN

BLEKINGEGATAN

Hotel Point

BJURHOLMSGATAN

BRÄNNERIGATAN

ÖSTGÖTAGATAN

PELIKAN

GOTLANDSGATAN

A
B
C

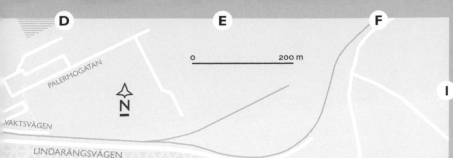

**D** **E** **F**

0 200 m

PALERMOGATAN

**N**

VAKTSVÄGEN

LINDARÄNGSVÄGEN

**I**

LINDARÄNGSVÄGEN

ELLJUSSPÅR

ELLJUSSPÅR

# ÖSTERMALM

## LADUGÅRDSGÄRDET

**2**

ELLJUSSPÅR

**KAKNÄSTORNET**

NS

VÅG

**3**

MÖRKA KROKEN

KAKNÄSVÄGEN

**TEKNISKA
MUSEET
(NATIONAL MUSEUM OF
SCIENCE AND TECHNOLOGY)**

smuseet
ce
eum)

DJURGÅRDSBRUNNSVÄGEN

**ETNOGRAFISKA
MUSEET
(MUSEUM OF ETHNOGRAPHY)**

HUNDUDDSVÄGEN

**4**

**DJURGÅRDSBRUNN**

**D** **E** **F**

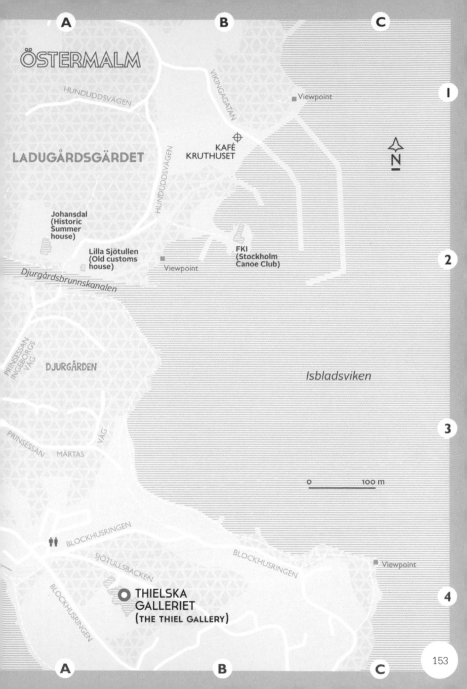

ÖSTERMALM

HUNDUDDSVÄGEN

LADUGÅRDSGÄRDET

Johansdal
(Historic
Summer
house)

Lilla Sjötullen
(Old customs
house)

Djurgårdsbrunnskanalen

DJURGÅRDEN

PRINSESSAN
INGEBORGS
VÄG

PRINSESSAN
MÄRTAS VÄG

BLOCKHUSRINGEN

SJÖTULLSBACKEN

BLOCKHUSRINGEN

BLOCKHUSRINGEN

VIKINGAGATAN

HUNDUDDSVÄGEN

KAFÉ
KRUTHUSET

FKI
(Stockholm
Canoe Club)

Isbladsviken

■ Viewpoint

■ Viewpoint

■ Viewpoint

N

○ THIELSKA
GALLERIET
(THE THIEL GALLERY)

0 ——— 100 m

A  B  C

1

2

3

4

NOSTALGIPALATSET

ACNE
ARCHIVE

TENNSTOPET

Stockholms
Improvisationsteater
(theatre)

Teatrestudio
Lederman
(theatre)

Aliasteatern
(theatre)

Teatre
Giljotin

Bio Capitol
(cinema)

Ibis
Stoc
Ode

Eastmanfont
(foun

SANKT ERIKSPLAN

Sankt Eriksplan

Arbetaren statue
(The Labourer)

VASAPARKEN

Sven-Harrys
Konstmuseum
(art museum)

Västra
Parken

Bonniers
Konsthall
(art gallery)

FALUGATAN

TORSGATAN

SANKT ERIKSGATAN

HÄLSINGEGATAN

FREJGATAN

KARLBERGSVÄGEN

N

0          100 m

SIGTUNAGATAN

GÄSTRIKEGATAN

HÄLSINGEGATAN

DALAGATAN

DALAGATAN

VÄSTMANNAGATAN

ODENGATAN

SANKT ERIKSGATAN

TORSGATAN

SANKT ERIKSPLAN

VÖLUNDSGATAN

ATLASGATAN

ATLASMUREN

TORSGATAN

TORSGATAN

EASTMANSVÄGEN

MEDEVIGATAN

OLIVECRONASV

HÄLSOBRUNNSGATAN

TORSGRÄND

VALL
SABBATS G

A          B          C

1

2

3

4

**A** Mosaiska Begravningsplatsen Aronsberg (Jewish cemetery)

Connect Hotel

ALSTRÖMERGATAN

**B**

FRIDHEMSGATAN

SANKT ERIKSGATAN

**BILJARDPALATSET**

**C** KLARASTRANDSLEDEN

Barnhusvikan

KUNGSHOLMS STRAND

IGELDAMMSGATAN

**1**

FLEMINGGATAN

KRONOBERGSGATAN

INEDALSGATAN

ÅNGSTRÖMSGATAN

POLHEMSGATAN

**VÄSTERMALMS GALLERIAN**

KUNGSHOLMEN

Hotel Aldoria

GRUBBENS GATA

*Grubbensparken*

MARIEBERGSGATAN

SANKT

ARBETARGATAN

GÖRANSGATAN

FLEMINGGATAN

PARKGATAN

*Tidningsläsarna statue*

**PHIL'S BURGER**

Laborate sculpture

KRONOBERGSGATAN

CELSIUSGATAN

**FRIDHEMSPLAN**

**2** DROTTNINGHOLMSVÄGEN

*Kronobergsparken*

POLHEMSGATAN

KUNGSHOLMSGATAN

Gosse med Urna statue (Boy with Urn)

Fridhemsplan Hotel

*Sysslomansparken*

**KUNGSHOLMEN**

BERGSGATAN

FRIDHEMSGATAN

KARLSVIKSGATAN

SANKT ERIKSGATAN

BALTZAR VON PLATENS GATA

HANTVERKARGATAN

RÅLAMBSHOVSLEDEN

NORR MÄLARSTRAND

PONTONJÄRGATAN

*Pontonjärparken*

**NATURKOMPANIET**

**3**

**RÅLAMBSHOVS PARKEN**

PONTONJÄRGATAN

NORR

POLHEMSGATAN

PONTONJÄRGATAN

PILGATAN

**Landstingshuset (City Council)**

*Rålambshovsparkens Amfiteater*

MÄLARSTRAND

**MÄLARPAVILJONGEN**

**4**

VÄSTERBRON

*Riddarfjärden*

N

0    200 m

**A**

**B**

**C**

# INDEX

## ABOUT THE AUTHOR

Becky first visited Stockholm as a toddler, on a trip to meet her maternal grandparents. Later, as a teen, she mastered enough of the language and geography to make an important daily pilgrimage to the local snack kiosk for chocolate. Becky will still go out of her way for a bar of Marabou mjölk choklad (milk chocolate), but several periods of living in Stockholm over the years have expanded her tastes and interests. These days, she never misses a chance to revisit her favourite paintings at the Modern Art museum, tuck into a bowl of fish stew in the basement of Hötorgshallen food court, stop for a fika (coffee break) in an old-fashioned cafe, play some pinball in an underground billiards hall, or walk along the city's many bridges and canals.

Becky has researched and written about Stockholm for Lonely Planet since 2004; she has written about family travel in Sweden for the *Independent*, and landscape as a character in Swedish literature for *The Bear Deluxe*. She also writes about hiking and camping in the Pacific North-west. When she's not travelling for work, Becky rides motorcycles with the Sang-Froid Riding Club in Portland, Oregon.

## ACKNOWLEDGEMENTS

Thanks first of all to fellow travel writer Carolyn Bain for suggesting my name for this project, and to Hardie Grant publisher Melissa Kayser and travel editor Megan Cuthbert for letting me take it on. Huge thanks to editor Alice Barker for her patient and careful work on the manuscript, and to designer Michelle Mackintosh and typesetter Megan Ellis for putting it all together. For helping me explore our favourite city yet again, thanks to Mom and Dad. For making the long trek with the family, thanks to Karl, Natalie and the kids. For perfect timing and providing a great excuse to play – not to mention the hostel jailbreak – thanks to Brenda Vitale and Jim Vaughey.

## PHOTO CREDITS

All images are © Becky Ohlsen, except the following:

Page vi centre Kajsas Fisk, lower-left Creative Commons/Magnus Ek, Oaxen Slip; 3 lower-right Livrustkammaren; 24–25 Operan; 26 lower and 27 top Kajsas Fisk; 38 lower Katja Halvorsson (Rosendals Tradgard); 39 lower Lena Granefelt (Rosendals Tradgard); 41 Oaxen Krog & Slip; 62–63 Barbro; 67 lower-right Debaser/Bar Brooklyn; 78 Creative Commons: 82–83 Strindbergsmuseet; 87 Flippin' Burgers; 88 top and lower Café Tranan; 92 top and lower Tekniska Museet, centre Anna Gerdén; 98 Djurgårdsbrunn; 114 top Vaxholms Stad, lower Jesper Wahlström; 115 top, right, and lower Vaxholms Stad, middle-left Jesper Wahlström; 118–119 Joel Ohlsen; 122 lower Soren Vilks, centre Joel Ohlsen, top Elias Gammelgård; 123 top Kungliga Hovstaterna, lower Alexis Daflos; 163 top Mike Russell, second Barbro, centre and lower Tranan.

Published in 2019 by Hardie Grant Travel,
a division of Hardie Grant Publishing

Hardie Grant Travel (Melbourne)
Building 1, 658 Church Street
Richmond, Victoria 3121

Hardie Grant Travel (Sydney)
Level 7, 45 Jones Street
Ultimo, NSW 2007

www.hardiegrant.com/au/travel

The maps in this publication incorporate data from

© OpenStreetMap contributors

OpenStreetMap is made available under the Open
Data Commons Open Database License (ODbL) by the
OpenStreetMap Foundation (OSMF):

http://opendatacommons.org/licenses/odbl/1.0/.
Any rights in individual contents of the database are
licensed under the Database Contents License:
http://opendatacommons.org/licenses/dbcl/1.0/

Data extracts via Geofabrik GmbH
https://www.geofabrik.de

A catalogue record for this
book is available from the
National Library of Australia

Stockholm Pocket Precincts
ISBN 9781741176285

10 9 8 7 6 5 4 3 2 1

**Publisher**
Melissa Kayser

**Senior editor**
Megan Cuthbert

**Project editor**
Alice Barker

**Proofreader**
Helena Holmgren

**Cartographer**
Emily Maffei

**Design**
Michelle Mackintosh

**Typesetting**
Megan Ellis

**Index**
Max McMaster

**Prepress**
Megan Ellis and Splitting Image Colour Studio

Printed and bound in China by LEO Paper Group

**Disclaimer:** While every care is taken to ensure
the accuracy of the data within this product, the
owners of the data (including the state, territory
and Commonwealth governments of Australia) do
not make any representations or warranties about
its accuracy, reliability, completeness or suitability
for any particular purpose and, to the extent
permitted by law, the owners of the data disclaim
all responsibility and all liability (including without
limitation, liability in negligence) for all expenses,
losses, damages (including indirect or consequential
damages) and costs which might be incurred as a
result of the data being inaccurate or incomplete in
any way and for any reason.

**Publisher's Disclaimers:** The publisher cannot
accept responsibility for any errors or omissions.
The representation on the maps of any road or
track is not necessarily evidence of public right of
way. The publisher cannot be held responsible for
any injury, loss or damage incurred during travel.
It is vital to research any proposed trip thoroughly
and seek the advice of relevant state and travel
organisations before you leave.

**Publisher's Note:** Every effort has been made
to ensure that the information in this book is
accurate at the time of going to press. The publisher
welcomes information and suggestions for correction
or improvement.